When Pr

WHEN PRETTY was UGLY!

Overcoming life's hideous moments to become who you were meant to be

DINAH REID

When Pretty was Ugly!

Copyright © 2020 by Dinah Reid

Printed in the United States of America

ISBN: 978-0-578-69267-8

The author has tried to recreate events, locales and conversations from her memories of them. In order to maintain their anonymity in some instances, names have been changed of individuals and places. The author may have changed some identifying characteristics and details such as physical properties, occupations and places of residence.

To order additional copies of this book, contact:

Dinah Reid
P.O. Box 1212
Salem, Virginia, 24153

dinahtreid@gmail.com

available at www.amazon.com

Book Production:
Marvin D. Cloud

I dedicate this book to everyone all over the world, but women in particular, who have suffered the pains of physical, sexual, and emotional abuse.

Acknowledgments

First, I give all honor to God Almighty and my Savior Jesus Christ for giving me the courage to share my life with others in order for them to get the help they need.

Next, this book is destined to be a legacy I will leave behind for my daughters, Krystal Scarborough and Korean Mills to share with my eight beautiful grandchildren.

I thank my husband, Reginald Reid for his love and patience during this process.

Contents

CHAPTER 1

The Year 1969

The year 1969 was a pivotal year in American history. The Rock "N" Roll group known as The Beatles, made their last public performance. France's super plane, the Concorde made its first test flight. Pontiac introduced its muscle car, the Firebird Trans Am. The music festival, Woodstock attracted over 350,000 rock fans, to a dairy farm in Bethel, New York. The Manson Family, a cult led by Charles Manson, murdered five people. Neil Armstrong and Edwin 'Buzz' Aldrin, astronauts aboard the Apollo 11 spaceship, became the first humans to explore the moon.

The year 1969 was also a turning point for me. My siblings and I played outside in the summer heat and entertained ourselves in order to not be in grown folks' faces when they had company. In Charlotte, North Carolina, adults lived by the adage, "Children should be seen and not heard," when in their presence. We soon discovered it was even better to not be seen. Every day, we made mud pies from the red clay dirt mixed with water also we played "Mommy and Daddy." That was an opportunity for us to mimic the actions we saw in our own household; fathers as they went to work, and mothers as they cooked dinner and cleaned house, etc.

"Come on! Make a tent!" someone yelled. "We can put a blanket over the chairs and make a house." Shortly afterwards, a pee-stained blanket became the roof of our playhouse. I can almost smell it today, mainly because that was the moment my life changed forever.

"Resa, you go in first and then I will come in after you," someone said. I was called Resa for short, but my name is Teresa. I went in and my playmate, Rosalyn said, "Now you lay down here and be the mama, and I will be the daddy."

Just like that, boom! I was pushed to the ground. I laid on my back, and took orders from another six or seven year old. That was the first time I played this new game that was apparently old hand to many of my friends.

Rosalyn was a neighbor's child my mom kept that summer in order for her mom to go to work. The next step in the process entailed my dress being pulled up. I know I must have had a confused look on my face as I laid there and stared up at the blue blanket while the sun roasted the pee smell in the air. Her actions frightened me. Why was I afraid of my playmate? To this day I do not know.

Rosalyn did what I later learned to be "hunching" as we say in the South. That's when you lay down and someone gets on top of you and move and press their private parts against yours. Now, there was something in me that knew this was not the right thing at my age, but what could I do? If I stopped playing and went inside, before I could say anything, I would get a whipping. In those days, when your mama said, "Y'all chaps go outside and play till I say come in," that's what you did.

As I laid there in a fogged-out daze, I felt shock, confusion, and disgust concerning what happened to me. I might have had an out-of-body experience because it felt like l looked down at myself, although the little girl on her back didn't seem like me.

Suddenly, I came back to reality when I heard my big sister, Lee, shout, "Rosalyn! What the hell are y'all doing with y'all little fast asses? Resa, get your tail up from there!"

I never imagined that first experience would have a bearing on me for the rest of my life. The house at 837 Holland Ave., was filled with many dysfunctional drunken guests and a stepfather who was a child molester to three of my older sisters. JT, as my mom, Bell, called her lover, would remain a constant in my life as my daddy for 18 years. Although he was my step-father, he was the only father I knew, therefore, I called him "Daddy."

The pains I suffered from childhood to adulthood prepared me for such a time as now. My life and destiny were at stake and the devil wanted to stop me from moving forward to keep the plans God had for my life unfulfilled. He tried many times to kill me. He started the day of my birth. Born with a hole in my heart and fluid on my brain,

3

the first attack was spoken out of the doctor's mouth. He told my mom, "Don't name her because she will be dead by the morning. If she lives, she will not walk or talk."

My birth would be symbolic to my life because I was born with a hole in my heart and fluid on my brain. God the Father cursed the mouth of Satan and the attacks Satan sent through my life. God interceded and intercepted many attacks on my life. The ones He allowed, turned out to be for my good.

The adversary did not know what God had in store for me when I was born on December 31, 1963, but I'm honored my mom did not believe the devil's report. Father God knew greater was coming behind me and I give all the glory and honor back to Him. Many times the devil tried to kill me because God cursed the words spoken over me by the doctor. God had prepared a table for me in the presence of my enemies because he knew what my life would be. Like the prophet Jeremiah, He knew me before I was formed and shaped in my mother's womb.

His second attack on my life came when I was two years-old. I found a bottle of aspirin and ate all of the tablets. I passed out and turned blue. God used my mom, Bell, to breathe into my mouth. She called, Tab, a taxi driver she knew, and he drove us to the hospital. My mom was in the back seat and she breathed life back in me. My life was spared again.

The third attack came when I was a toddler. My mother noticed me as I chewed on something. She asked, "What's in your mouth?" She saw it was an old razor blade and quickly packed my mouth with Vaseline. She took the razor blade out and it was a miracle that my mouth wasn't cut up. Shortly, thereafter, at the age of five, the fourth attack took place. One morning, a glass jar filled with bleach sat on the kitchen counter. My mom had washed clothes earlier, and she left it there. I thought it was juice. I picked it up and drank all of it. I felt a burning sensation move down my throat but I continued to drink. Rita called Poison Control and the person on the phone said to give me a stick of butter and sherbet frozen dessert to eat. In short order, I was fine.

The fifth attack came when I was eight. I roller-skated down the street and a rock caught under my wheel. I tripped, fell, and bit my tongue in half. When I went into the house crying with blood everywhere, my mom dropped the phone. She stuffed a towel in my mouth and called a cab to transport me to Charlotte Memorial Hospital. They sewed it back together. Again it was a victory for the Holy Spirit. The devil thought he had me, but God knew differently.

The first five years of my life presented three unsuccessful attacks brought on my life by the adversary and two more at the age of eight, but my God brought me out of all of them. I didn't know it then, but I know now that Psalm 34:19 KJV states, "Many are the afflictions of the righteous but God delivered him out of them all."

Every time the devil tried to close my mouth I would live to fight another day. Through heartbreak and pain, and the many times my heart was stomped on and my hopes shattered, it was for His purpose. It wasn't for nothing. I spent most of my life trusting the wrong people and like that hole in my heart I was born with, the heart breaks in my life were consistent.

At 837 Holland Ave., too much happened for any child to have lived through. I watched my mama become a weekend drunk and lived with an alcoholic stepdad who was also a child molester. It's no wonder I grew up defensively and did not make friends easily. I didn't trust anyone. Maybe like the late Michael Jackson, I could have befriended a rat, named him "Ben," and kept him for a pet. Lord knows the rats in our area were the size of cats. They would invade our cramped, two-bedroom duplex whenever they wanted to, until somebody caught and killed them.

Our neighborhood was crazy. One time our neighbor, Mr. John, was shot in the face and the bullet came out of his mouth after my mama slapped him on the back a few times. Other times seem crazy when I look back at them, but that was our normal. For example, the family would often sit on the back porch in the summer time and eat yellow surplus grits and canned stew meat. My older sisters hung our clothes on the line and in the winter, they would be stiff as a board. My sisters would take big sticks and beat the ice off of the clothes before they took them down. There was a wide creek in the back of our house that my two younger brothers and I played in. We caught rollie pollie bugs, (the ones that would roll up in a tight ball when disturbed) crayfish, and silverfish that swam in the creek.

Every morning, we put our mattresses outside in the sun to dry because the night before, someone, usually Vest, would pee in the bed. That would make the little red "chinch" bugs come out and bite us. I hated waking up from a sound sleep to scratch my legs until they bled. Vest was the mischievous little brother with bucked teeth who couldn't stand to get his hair combed, but played in the grass all the time.

When I was six and he was seven, he played detective and took a bobby pin out my hair. He convinced me to go inside a neighbor's house. He picked the lock and in the kitchen, food sat on the stove. We sat at the table, ate the lady's food and drank her orange juice. Our friend, E. Orange was a neighbor who lived across the street from us. He walked by, saw us and threatened that he would tell if we didn't share it with him. We shared the food with him and he told on us anyway.

Another time, the bullies packed our clothes full of grass and tied us on the ground. They took turns hitting Vest and I. Because of the grass, it turned out to be the worse itching we ever had.

Like most children, we also played Cowboys and Indians. We ran around the house with a twine rope in an attempt to capture one another like a cowboy would rope a calf. One day, Vest had the rope around me and held the two ends as we ran. I fell and the rope got caught up between my legs. When he pulled it, it sliced the back of my legs like butter. My legs were sore to the point I could not bend them. It was hard to sit and stand, but I eventually made it through.

My second instance of acting out sexually occurred around the same age, and on another hot, scorching, summer day. My youngest brother, Vest, took me by the hand and led me up a hill to a patch of tall, thick, grass. I don't remember exactly what happened, but when we came out of the tall grass, I was as puzzled and confused as when Rosalyn was on top on me.

My mom spent her weekends at the liquor house with JT while I stayed at home and witnessed the craziness around me. Often, though, I was at the liquor house with her. There, I witnessed everything from mean dogs barking in the yard, to big money card games on playing tables, souse meat, crackers, pickled eggs, pigs feet, corn liquor, chicken "wangs," and fried fish, along with grown-ups who danced to the music that came from the piccolo machine.

"Hop, hop, hop. Baby do the frog. Resa, do the frog for your daddy," JT would say.

I would crouch down as I listened to the "hole in the wall" music. I would put on my best performance for my daddy's friends because I knew he really liked this dance and would get real happy as I hopped around on the floor for them. As I look back on it now, they probably got some kind of twisted thrill as they watched my legs and crotch area as I hopped across the floor.

I have to admit though, as I watched the gamblers, the fights, the card tables as they were knocked over, and heard the drunken screams of profanity, the action at the liquor house was better than playing with my dolls or riding my bicycle. It was a welcome respite from life at our apartment and what I knew and didn't know. For example, I didn't have a clue that my oldest sisters, Rita, Patty, and Lee, were regularly molested by my daddy.

Being the youngest girl of 11 siblings, was not easy for me. However, the baby girl that my overprotective mother and overbearing brothers were suppose to protect from the evilness of this world, fell into dysfunction. I was the larvae inside of the silk cocoon they should have kept from hurt, harm, and danger. It's funny how I did not end up an alcoholic, a drug addict, or a child molester, as a product of my past. Yet, in many ways I still did not clearly get away without any scars.

Rita, who is now deceased, told me he molested her and she told my mom about it. She later recanted out of fear when the Department of Social Services showed up to investigate, probably because she didn't want to be separated from our mom. Patty said my dad would play with her breasts and give her lunch money for school, all right under my mom's nose. Lee told me he kissed her in the mouth and when she told my mom about it, she refused to believe it.

There was one incident my siblings and I witnessed to support Rita's account. At this time, there were 10 of us cramped into a two-bedroom apartment; two adults and eight children. When it came time to sleep, we had two rollaway beds, a fold-out couch, and two sets of bunk beds. One day, my mom told us to stay in the bedroom we all shared while she ran an errand across the street to a neighbor's house.

"Y'all, I'll be right back. Don't go into the other room where your daddy is because he is drunk and asleep."

All of us obeyed except Rita. My mother went down the hall and pretended to leave. We watched as Rita exited our room and went across the hall into my parent's room and into our daddy's arms. She embraced him in a long, lip-locked, heated kiss. We were shocked. My mom had become suspicious at some point along the way. She tip-toed back down the hall, opened the bedroom door, and to her surprise, her man and her daughter were embraced in a kiss.

"JT! Rita! What the hell is going on?"

My daddy dropped back on the bed and pretended to be *extremely* drunk. It was like he didn't know what happened. His performance was worthy of an Oscar. Rita stood in the middle of the floor, wrung her hands and cried. My mom put my daddy out of our apartment—for a short while.

After some time had passed, Rita became pregnant and eventually gave birth to a daughter. My mother always thought JT was the father. This was never proven. It was a long-standing rumor in my family. Coincidentally, at the same time my mother was also pregnant and my sister, Janet, was pregnant.

Years, later in 1998, Rita told me she would go to her grave and never tell anybody who was the father of two of her children. I asked her point-blank if our stepdad was the father of her first-born, but she would only say she would never tell anyone. I left it alone. After she gave birth to my niece, Heather, Rita moved out a year later and married David Lee, her twins' daddy. My mom lost her baby due to a miscarriage and Janet had a daughter.

There were many drunken fights between my mother and my dad regarding his cheating and the possibility of him messing around with her other children.

One time, my parents had a heated argument. My mom picked me up by the arm and carried me into the bathroom where we hid from my father. She placed me on her lap as she sat on the toilet. I heard a loud bang. He fired a bullet into the bathroom.

Amid a loud outburst and screams, my mother said, "Oh, lord, y'all daddy just shot me!"

I was still on my mom's lap and I cried in disbelief as the bullet casing hit the bathtub then rolled across the floor. It stopped when it hit my mom's toe. I was terrified by the sight of blood on the floor. I thought my mom was indeed shot. The loud boom from the pistol my dad waved around pierced my eardrums. I was gripped with paralyzing fear.

All of my siblings grabbed what they could and beat him to a bloody pulp. They used broomsticks, pots and pans, while my younger brothers bit him around the ankles and beat his feet with high heel shoes. Janet threw a long-blade butcher's knife at him that stuck in the door frame as he ran out of the door.

My brother, Fred and Janet fussed and fought all the time. They were like oil and water. I would be right there. From the safety of my tricycle, I watched every bit of the action. One day, they got into it real bad and Fred locked the screen door to keep Janet out. She picked up a brick, threw it through the screen door into the house and put a hole in Mama's hi-fi. Probably the worst scene happened the time my mama had a miscarriage in the kitchen as I stood in the hallway. She sweated and wiped her face. Then ... Blam! She hit the floor and laid there in a pool of blood. My brother-in-law, Doug, Brenda's husband, helped her until she was carried away in an ambulance.

I eventually met my two nephews who belonged to my oldest brother, Danny. I would go over to their house in Double Oaks and play that new hunching game with my youngest nephew.

Sins of Life

There are many sins we encounter in our daily lives, whether in deed or thought we commit them.

Some of us know exactly what we are getting ourselves into before it happens.

However, we hold on to them because we enjoy the comfort that we think they bring.

Our sins of life are much like gum chewing. Don't we all know that gum, like sin, is sweet to taste but it's texture is elastic. We know how the chew is long and repetitive, but we'll chew for hours and hours like the sins of life for years and years, hours or days.

If we are smart and meditate with God, we will chew on sin for a short time because the sweet taste is gone away, like gum when it has lost its flavor.

Others are not so wise; they will keep the gum in their mouths continuing to chew the sins of life. As followers of Christ, let us not continue to chew on our sins, but to release them into the trash where they belong.

—Dinah Reid

Chapter 2

Moving on Up

A couple of years passed by and in 1971 we moved a few streets over to another duplex on MacArthur Ave. I was excited because the house was not as crowded since some of my older siblings had moved out. Perhaps with less mouths to feed, the stress level lessened and we had a semblance of a regular family. One time, my dad gave me a tricycle, a bike with training wheels, a baby doll that could walk, and another one that wore a nurse's outfit complete with a medical bag. My mom bought me skates and a 12-speed bicycle for Christmas along with board games.

Living a carefree life at the tender age of eight would soon be another disappointing blow of promiscuous sexual activity with another playmate. This time it was with a nine-year-old boy. Earl lived on the street we moved from. He was a classmate, but he was one of the meanest of the children we played with on the block. I believe my brothers, B-Baby and Vest, were afraid of him because he was a bully. He would throw rocks at us, push children down, fight them, and take their candy, etc.

One day, my brothers and I played outside. I was a tomboy and I stuck to them because we were close in age. I played in the woods, climbed trees, and played in the creeks to catch crayfish and earth worms. Earl came around to play with us and to show off his new bicycle. He was spoiled. We were always happy to play with his things when he would let us because he had the best toys, but he was still a bully. One on my brothers asked to ride his bicycle.

The next thing I knew, leaves crunched around me as the damp black earth was beneath my bottom parts. Earl said," I will let all of you ride if you let me do the nasty with your sister." I loved my brothers and would do anything for them.

"Ouch, ouch, ouch. It hurts. Stop, I don't want to do this anymore!" I shouted.

No one could hear me because I was in the woods with Earl. Vest watched out for adults, and B-Baby rode his bike. This was the worst pain I had ever felt in my private area. I tried to look down to see what he was doing. I couldn't see but I felt something move in and out of my vagina. It might have been a stick. Or maybe it was his finger. I remembered my white underwear was stained with the black dirt and dried up leaves. When it was over, we all took turns and rode Earl's bike like nothing had happened.

This was Resa, as everyone called me. "She's so pretty. She's so cute. She's got dimples. She's a beautiful little girl, Bell." I sure did not feel any of those things. My self-esteem went down the drain. The darkness of my heart felt as black as the dirt I had laid on. This accounted for years of depression. Family, boyfriend, and spousal abuse followed.

As a result of this incident and others, I hated the words "pretty" or "cute" and decided not to accept myself as being anything but dirty and less than others. I also decided to not show emotion when I was happy. I knew it wouldn't be long before something dark would come to destroy anything I felt good about. On the other hand, even though I felt worthless, I pushed myself to do things for people in order to be accepted by them. I wanted them to give me love in return. I think this is why I became a caregiver later in life—to be rewarded for doing for others who could not do for themselves. Also, my need for love made it hard to say "no," even if I felt uncomfortable doing something in order to fit in and feel loved. Sometimes it meant doing something I knew was wrong. "Pretty" was a word I used to associate with being superior to others. It was not something I ever wanted to be because I felt I was only a regular girl who tried to figure out life. In return, I wanted to be included.

The truth of the matter was, I was smart, attractive, and talented, but I had no one to show me there was nothing wrong with self-love and believing in my own achievements. I wasn't taught it didn't mean it was wrong to display positive outward expressions.

Later that day, after Earl's assault, I had to use the bathroom. When I tried to urinate, I felt an excruciating, burning, stinging, throbbing pain in my vagina. I screamed as the urine went down my legs onto the bathroom floor and the pain I felt would not let up.

Janet came in the bathroom and asked, "What's wrong?"

"It hurts when I try to pee," I said.

Janet yelled, "Why are you hurting down there? Who been messing with you? JT's nasty ass? I will kill him. Tell me the truth. You know it was him."

I cried even more because I told her my daddy did nothing to me. "It was a boy named Earl."

Strangely, although my step-daddy was a pedophile, to my knowledge, he never molested me. The next day, my sister took me to the clinic in the back of Charlotte Memorial Hospital to get treated for sexual assault. Dr. Williams was a black doctor and a pretty lady. She talked with my sister and they both tried to convince me to say my daddy did this to me.

I left the clinic with diapers and two packs of some sort of sulfur solution to put in the water for me to soak in. I was humiliated and ashamed of myself because I had to wear diapers to school in the third grade. I couldn't hold my pee.

Still, when I hung out with Vest and B-Baby, some of the best childhood times were forged. We got along the best because we were still in our innocence and had not been corrupted by the world. I played in the yard and cut flips and went to the candy lady's house to get the penny cookies and candies, but I liked the rope bubblegum, candy lipstick, and candy cigarettes the best.

Some days we sat on the porch and watched guys as they rode their horses. They often let us pet them. Other days they raced up and down the street and this scared me to death.

Another harrowing time happened during another argument between my mama and daddy. He threatened her and this time I saw terror in her eyes. Danny walked through the door, grabbed my dad by his neck and threw him up in the air. His head hit the ceiling and he landed on the floor in a crumpled heap. It was a long time before he put his hands on her again.

Our neighborhood had more action than any movie theater. Once, B-Baby and Patty left the house to walk to school. In no time flat they ran back to the house. They said they saw a dead man who lay in the grass. Sure enough he was face up with his eyes open. We didn't have any idea who he was or how he got there. Three big dogs ate away at his guts.

Another time, B-Baby came home from school. He acted funny and talked out of his mind. No one knew what to think of it.

He said, "Mama take that belt over there and tear his ass up."

She knew something was wrong with him and they took him to the hospital. Through various tests and questioning, the doctors determined he had been given candy laced with some kind of narcotic. Neither the police nor anyone else found out who had poisoned him.

Being a child raised in an abusive household also made me angry and unable to trust anyone who was nice to me or close to me. Every time I did trust them, they would let me down. That caused me to develop feelings of rage. Like the character, Sophia, played by Oprah Winfrey in the movie, "The Color Purple," all my life I had to fight. It made me bitter. Why would people always pick me to assault? I had to live with the feeling of resentment for years.

I learned early in my life not to trust anyone because of the bullying I endured by some of my elementary playmates, particularly females. There were a few schoolyard fights that set the tone for me concerning how I felt about girls. My intuition to trust my own instinct when it comes to females proved to be right. The children would always bully me because of the way I dressed. I was raised on welfare and I could not afford clothing like most of my other classmates.

In 1970, North Carolina State integrated the school system and placed black and white students together. The idea was to educate everyone fairly in order for black children to receive the same treatment as white children and not feel like outcasts. One day in math class, a white student called me "A dumb-ass nigger," because I missed a math equation. I don't think the teacher heard her. That feeling of rage came over me. In my first-grade mind, I had to make her pay for how she humiliated me in front of everyone.

During recess, the class waited in a single-file line to go to the play area. I broke off switches from a tree like my mom whipped us with and used them on my classmate. I called her a "cracker" and said I would beat her white ass. We both fell to the ground. I screamed and hollered from rage and she screamed and hollered from pain. The switches left big red welts on her leg. My teacher came to her rescue and took me to the office where they called her parents and my mom. They wanted to expel me from school for the entire year.

When her parents and my mom met, it was discovered that their child had called me a "dumb-ass nigger." All charges were dropped and I remained in school. Her parents shouted and screamed they never used such words. They couldn't fathom where their daughter had picked that up. Apparently, they took her out of Hidden Valley School because I do not recall seeing her again.

After being met with much adversity in my young life, pretty little Teresa felt nothing but ugly. Ages 10 to 15 were painful for me also because I spent most of my days physically fighting my brothers, sisters, and neighborhood children. Vest, and I were close; I took up for him when we were five or six years of age, but when he reached age 10, he began to use me as his punching bag. I never knew what made him change on me but it happened on several occasions. One time in particular, we fought over something minor. We were in the kitchen and Vest, the one I loved dearly, picked me up in the air and threw me to the kitchen floor. The impact burst my mouth open and cracked my teeth. I probably should have received stitches, but I didn't. I got up from the kitchen floor and grabbed a long barbecue fork and stabbed him in the back as he ran out the back door. My oldest sister, Debra, came down to our house and cleaned my mouth.

When my mom came home from clubbing with her sisters, and was told about the fight, nothing happened to my brother. However, she criticized me for stabbing him. She said, "You could have killed him."

I listened to her in disbelief. My mouth was swollen and still stung with pain. But my injury didn't count. There was always a question in my mind *why don't my mother like me?* She always found a way to explain away everything that happened to me.

In third grade, Margie White would make me her target every day after school. I was her project to beat on. At three o'clock, when it was time to catch the bus and go home she started on me. I would flee into the restroom and nervously cry because I did not want to face her. As soon as she would board the bus, she would not rest until she found me and taunted me.

She would say, "Teresa McQuiller, what are you looking at with your big ole head? You think you cute?"

Then she would pull my hair, pinch me, or smack me upside my head. At the same time, she would curse. I tried to be nice to her. If I had anything like a snack, crayons, or pencils, I would give it to her. She was a big girl, at least for her age. Her size alone terrified me. Plus, she was in the fifth grade. I could never figure out why she did not like me. Every day, when I got off the bus, I would cry and run all the way home to tell my mom she had picked on me again.

My mom finally had enough of it and she said to me, "If you go to school tomorrow and come home telling me this girl bullied you, I will whip your tail."

The next day when I boarded the bus, Margie started her daily ritual; a pinch here, a slap there. I sat there and cried. The bus driver asked her to stay in her seat and to leave me alone but she would not. I thought about the whipping I would get when I got home. Then, a few more miles down the road, suddenly, there was a change of events. Margie kicked me on the ankle with the heel of her boots. The pain was excruciating. Before I knew it, I was on top her. I beat the hell out of her and when I finished, she had a bloodied nose and she screamed for her life.

The bus driver was shocked and she said, "I knew one day that little girl was going to beat your ass and I'm glad."

It was like a bolt of lightning had hit me and I could not stop. All of the pent up rage I had been holding inside all year was unleashed on her. The bus driver stopped the bus and pulled me off Margie. It took this one time to stop her. After that day she never bothered me again and I was relieved not to get a whipping by my mom.

When I got older, I understood bullies have a need to be the center of attention. They are weak and unsure of themselves. They must bring others down in order to feel worthy. When someone is targeted by bullies, for most of their life, they will not trust anyone. I didn't trust girls or women. I drew closer to males because they seemed to understand me better, and they weren't two-faced, jealous, or intimidated by me. I felt relaxed and welcomed.

Another time I was on the basketball court during recess and this big girl, Pam Caulton, was upset with me over the ball. She must have been about five foot ten inches tall and she had long, claw-like fingernails that she kept in a jar. This though, was the funniest fight I had. Picture me as I jumped up and down like a bunny rabbit and tried to avoid her long arms.

Once I got to middle school, I had an encounter with the eighth grade school bully named Sandra Blade. School-age girls at Barr Street Middle School shook in their boots because of Sandra. She singled me out to fight however, because all of the children in the gym laughed about an event that happened in the back of the bus. Twenty children must have laughed that day but she picked me to fight during the lunch break.

I was afraid of her because of the stories everyone told me about her. Her reputation preceded her. I went to the girls' restroom and prayed, "Father God, you know I didn't do anything to this girl. If she fights me during lunch break, please give me the wisdom of Solomon and the strength of Samson to carry it out."

When it was time to go to lunch, it seemed like everyone had heard of the fight that was supposed to take place between Sandra and I. My heart beat fast and my palms sweated. I wanted this moment to pass me by.

As we entered the schoolyard, I noticed none of the girls whom I thought were my friends supported me. I turned around and in amazement, they all stood around Sandra, the bully, like they were best friends or allies.

One girl said, "I'll bet you all a dime that Sandra Blade cannot beat Teresa."

I thank God for Jesus. He had a ram in the bush prepared for me. Little did I know one of my teachers, Mrs. Wilson, watched the whole episode play out and witnessed that I tried to walk away from the confrontation. The rest was a blur.

After the fight was over, I learned I had beat this girl out of her clothes, tore her bra off, and blackened both of her eyes. The rage and fear took over during the fight when I heard my classmates say she would cut my face. I knew it was possible because her family was known in town as being bullies. When we got to the principal's office, he was prepared to suspend both of us for five days.

However, Mrs. Wilson walked in and said, "I will put my teaching license on the line for McQuiller. Mr. Ben, you will not suspend her. I saw the whole incident play out. Sandra is a classroom bully who often come to class late. I have had enough of her behavior in my classroom."

God took care of me on the schoolyard and in the principal's office. Mr. Ben changed his mind and did not suspend me. I was able to stay in school. Again, my decision not to trust females had not failed me. Once more I learned not to befriend them or get too close to them because they stung like a bee and bit like a serpent. Some of the girls on the schoolyard I had played with, spent nights at their house, and joked around with, but when I needed their support the most, they weren't there for me.

I had an uphill battle that consisted of always having to fight another neighborhood bully, S. Miles. She was the female version of Earl. She was mean as a snake in a pit. "Viper" would be a mild way to describe her, if you asked me.

This girl was my neighbor and friend. We played together well when we first moved to Pardue Street Apartments in 1974. She and I would play and eat at each other's house and sometimes, I would help her clean up. Then, one day out the blue, the beatings started. They happened almost every day for four years. S. Miles would wait for me every chance she got or where ever she saw me to pick a fight. It became a regular occurrence. Like the weather, I never knew what type of climate I would face from day to day. My trust was broken again, and for years, I struggled in adulthood because I never knew why my friend turned on me.

I made up my mind to do something with my life and escape a background of drunken arguments, sexual molestation, and drug addiction.

I Am

I am from above and not from beneath.

I am warm, beautiful, and glowing in uniqueness.

I am able to make all things grow.

I give life and nutrients to everything.

I go away sometimes, and then I come back around. The greatness of my glow can't stay present in order for things to grown.

For I am just like the sun that shines, and I come from above and not from beneath for I am "God Almighty from whom all blessings flow.

—Dinah Reid

CHAPTER 3

Pardue

Growing up in Pardue in the 70s, I saw my share of physical abuse. Many of the men who lived there would beat their women until they were black and blue. Once, I sat on my porch and chilled with my neighbors. One of them sat in a wooden chair besides me. Her boyfriend came around the corner and saw her sitting on her aunt's porch without his permission. He drew back his hand and hit her so hard she fell out of the chair. Then he stomped her with his platform shoes. By the way, she already had a broken arm. This couple fought all the time. People finally blocked them out of their minds. It wasn't a big deal. Then, one day the beating stopped. Her abuser was dead. Someone said he came home drunk, fell down the stairs, and broke his neck. We never knew the full story, but the rumor was she pushed him down the stairs.

Across the street, lived another couple who fought all the time. The guy would beat this lady only because he felt like it. Most the time, as soon as he got home, he would drag her out of the house and beat her in front of the neighbors.

Once, he dragged her by her head and her knees hit the ground as he punched her in the mouth and knocked out several of her teeth. Her mouth bled profusely.

The men from these two families beat their women all the time. It didn't matter whether they were the ones they lived with or the ones they whored around in the streets with. Meanwhile, most of the children ran around dusty and dirty. We played in the red, dusty sand on the side of my apartment complex in the blazing sun. A couple of the games were double-dutch, and hop-scotch. We also roller-skated, raced, and played soft ball. At other times, we picked crab apples, plums, or went to swim at the neighborhood pools.

Some of the little girls who should have spent their time playing, were too busy having sex and making babies as early as the age of 12. One of the girls I knew had five children by age 19. By the time some of the girls made it to middle and high school, they had been molested by teachers, staff members, and older classmates.

Many girls got excited about going to places we called the campground, backstreet, 747, Southside Park, and the hill. These were dirty, seedy-looking places they hung out at, to find boyfriends or men period, who apparently were in high demand. It seemed like there were 10 men to every woman. The girls and women spent time in knock-down, drag-out, fights over them. If one was lucky enough to get an engagement ring, it was like hitting the million dollar jackpot because the girl that did was almost considered as being royalty. The goals of the women were low because they looked forward to growing up and getting married, but the men looked forward to seeing how many females they could screw and how many babies they could make out of wedlock.

Growing up in the Pardue Street Apartments, the generational curse that lead our sexual tendencies and plagued our family had not skipped a beat. I was cute, pretty, energetic, had a nice figure and smile that lit up a heart. This prettiness got me in a great deal of trouble from my brother-in-law, cousins, and boys in the community who came after me. It's a wonder I felt any beauty at all. When they looked at me, they never saw me. They only saw the package and the smile that hid behind the pain of rejection and sexual abuse.

I was around 14 or 15 when a family member fondled my breasts. I went to Debra's house to use the phone for my mother when it took place. I talked on the phone, and tried to mind my own business when my brother-in-law, Hamilton, came into the kitchen. He called my name a few times, then walked up on me and squeezed both of my breasts with his hands. I froze stiff, like a block of ice. I was in shock. When I snapped out of it, I dropped the phone and ran out of the house. I told Janet and my mother what happened.

Later that day, when Debra, learned of it she said, "From now on, I don't want anybody coming up to my house to use the phone when I'm not home. My husband, Hamilton, is a whore. I know it and I love him."

After this happened, I noticed my sister kept her distance from me and I felt the tension in the air. To this day, we never spoke of this again ... it remains as a pink elephant in the room. The feeling I had when this happened was Debra and her daughter blamed me for the assault because according to them, "as fast as I was, I must have done something."

Pardue had a bad reputation. This was the place you came to if you wanted an easy lay, drinks, or drugs. I was too ashamed to tell anybody that did not already know, I lived there. If they found out, they would single me out and ask me for sex, too. Around ten teenagers I grew up never had sex and never got pregnant, and I'm proud to say I was one of them. B-Baby didn't get the memo because there was a time he beat me something awful because of a lie he heard on the street.

He was downtown hanging around on the hill with some of his fellows when they joked around about the number of girls they had sex with. One of the guys said he had sex with me and B-Baby believed it. That evening he came in the house in a rage and beat me and called me a fast-ass.

When I protested, he said, "Shut the hell up before I really beat your ass."

I screamed, but no one came to my rescue. About a week later, he caught the boy who started the rumor and beat him up until he told him the truth. My brother came home and tried to apologize to me, but I didn't want to hear it. B-Baby made me his breakfast, lunch, and dinner abuse person if he had a bad day. He picked me out to terrorize whenever he felt like it. He experimented with drugs like acid, cocaine, marijuana, and heroin, but we did not know it.

When I was 15, B-Baby came back to Patty's house from the club with some of his friends. He was high on marijuana and acid. I was asleep on Patty's sofa and he blew marijuana up my nose. He wanted to see how I would react if I got a "contact" in my sleep. He blew the smoke up my nose and I awakened with a scream. I coughed and cried because I could not breathe and it burned my throat. His friends laughed and pointed at me. Again, I told my mother and she did nothing regarding the incident but blew it off like always.

When I was 18, my mom was in the hospital. I was home and it was a sunny day. That summer, life was great for me. The day started out beautiful. I ate breakfast, cleaned up, and went outside for the day's events. Around 1 p.m., I came in the house with my friend, Nikki, to get something to drink. On the kitchen counter sat a clear glass of ice water. If I could turn back the hands of time, and go back to that day, I would have never drank that glass of ice water. After I quenched my thirst, I received one of the worst assaults of my life. Before I could put the glass on the table to explain to B-Baby why I drank it, I received a slap and a punch. Then his hands went around my throat and he choked me.

"Why did you drink my damn water? You are too damn fast! You had no business fucking with my shit!"

The beating continued as I screamed, "I can make you some more ice water!"

Of course he never heard me, or he didn't care. He beat me until I ended up on the floor on my hands and knees as I tried to get away from him. He kicked me so hard on my tailbone I had his shoeprint on my hip. Nikki ran across the street to get Rita and Patty.

They broke up the fight and asked, "Are you all right?" I had his whole handprint on the side of my face. Blue and black marks were around my neck, not to mention the shoe mark on my back side. Vest came home after he heard about what happened. He wanted to fight B-Baby, but he ran out of the house before the police came. When the police arrived, they said I could swear out a warrant on him. I intended to do that, but before I could get a ride to press the charges, my mother called me from the hospital. My brother had made a beeline there and he told her I called the police on him. She talked me out of pressing charges.

"You shouldn't call the police on your brother. That's not right."

I don't know why I listened to her and did nothing. Mainly it was because my mother was the dominating and controlling matriarch of our household. What she said, went, and she ruled with an iron fist.

The last fight B-Baby and I had was when I was 22. That beating happened because I did not want to babysit Patty's children while she went on a date. Patty and I argued because I did not want to keep her children. As we argued, he ironed his clothes and I washed dishes. Out of nowhere, a huge slap came across my face. I fell to the floor and as I got up, I tried to get a knife to cut him. He stopped me by beating me further down.

He said, "Shut up, bitch!"

My nose bled and I cried. *If I could get to that hot iron I would show him something.*

When I grabbed the iron, my mom sat on me and told him to run.

She said, "You cannot hit your brother with that hot iron and burn him!"

I yelled out, "I hate you! Why are you always beating on me? I wish you were dead."

Six months later, he died on the streets of Charlotte. I felt guilty I told him I wished he were dead because when he died, it hurt me terribly. I felt like I spoke death on him. I made sure to never say that to anyone else. We learned later he died of cold turkey withdrawals. He often did what's called speed balling. He mixed cocaine and heroin together and shot the mixture in his veins.

Once I asked him, "Why do you shoot up?"

He said, "I liked the way both drugs make me feel." The cocaine made him feel up and the heroin made him feel mellow. When he used them at the same time, it gave him an epic high.

The only person in my life who I felt loved me was Lee. I loved her with all my heart. She laughed and joked with me and came to my defense many times. Once she stopped my cousin, Stan, when he tried to rape me. We read books together, drew pictures, colored, played jackstones, and ate snacks together. She was also the one I told when I had my first real sexual experience, but her favorite thing for me to do for her was sing. Her whole face shined brightly. I sang even if I were out of tune. I know for a fact she loved me dearly and I miss her. She's been with the Lord since January 2015, and I know she is looking down and smiling as I continue my life's journey.

There were only a few times I was happy as a child. One was during the summers when I went to my Grandma Henrietta's house in Heath Springs, SC, on the back of my daddy's truck. She lived about 20 minutes away. This little town, named after the company Heath & Springs, has less than 1000 residents even now. Spending time with my grandma was always fun because she would fix delicious desserts including, pies and biscuits. I loved drinking the well water out of the tin cups she provided. I also enjoyed picking pecans and blackberries.

One time, when my granny baked biscuits in the kitchen, some of the children in the neighborhood messed with me and Vest. We told their mother but she didn't care.

I said, "I'm going to tell my grandma."

She said, "Tell your damn grandma."

We went inside and told her what happened. The lady next door cussed and fussed at my granny and told her to come out to the street. Granny did not say a word. She dusted her hands off on her apron then like a champion prize-fighter, she gave the lady two punches and she fell to the ground while dust balls rose up around her. She sat in the middle of the road and cried. Granny turned around, walked back to her kitchen, and baked the rest of the biscuits.

In the summer of 1978, I rode my bike to my sister's house without a care in this world. As long as I was home before the street lights came on, I was good. Janet bought me candy and listened to her old school music as she smoked weed. I ate onions and potatoes. My niece, Etta, was close to my age and we had fun when we played together, but we sometimes fought for attention from Janet. Other times, I helped my sister fix bottles for my little nephew, Wally.

Janet could out cuss any drunk sailor on his best day then she would switch and read the Bible to us. She made me learn John 3:16, "For God so loved the world, that he gave his only begotten Son, that whosoever believeth in him should not perish, but have everlasting life."

I saw a miracle get performed on her when I was 10 years old. She was sick and in a lot of pain. She cried a lot and her feet curled up. She prayed and asked me to believe with her. She held my hand while she cried out to God. I peeked at her and in amazement, I saw her feet straighten out. I said, "Look, Janet. God healed your feet."

Also at 15, my first dream vision came into a reality after I awakened. The night before, I dreamed that my sister, Debra's old apartment caught fire and neither the maintenance man nor my brother could get into the apartment to help people get out. The firemen broke the upstairs' window, went in and retrieved a baby, however, the infant was dead. The next morning, as my family and I ate breakfast, we heard people on the outside yell and scream.

"Hey, there is an apartment on fire! Somebody get help!" one of the voices said.

We ran outside to see what happened and to everyone's amazement the fire played out precisely as my dream.

Spiders and Their Webs

Spiders are some of the most unique and clever little creatures which god has made. They can be deadly as well as artful in their craft of web making. They can form many different shapes and sizes all which are beautiful and skillfully made.

Insects are sometimes attracted to these webs when they are following another path. While traveling on their journey, the insect lands on the spider's web. It is quickly trapped and devoured by the enemy spider.

We as human beings are distracted as well. We become separated from Christ while on our spiritual paths. So many times we stop along the way to talk and listen to every kind of doctrine or belief. Many of these conversations are not in the will of God or our spirit.

Soon, we find ourselves just like the insects in life, trapped. For we have eventually stepped upon the deceitful spider's web only to be destroyed and consumed. While on our walk with Christ, let us not be as the insect, a wanderer. Let us instead listen with our hearts and hear with our spirits to the direction in which we should travel.

—Dinah Reid

CHAPTER 4

The Matriarch

Bell was the leader of our family and what she said was written in stone. We did what she told us to do, especially me. I grew up loving her, but I was terrified of her at the same time. My mother was at least six foot tall and she had big, wide hands and big feet. When she hit you, it felt like you had been jabbed by a professional boxer. I knew early on not to cross her in any way. Bell could dress; she would be sharp as a tack in her hat, pocketbook, and boots to match. The cane she carried was made of brown oak. It had a smooth finish to it. Inside her purse she carried a pistol and was not afraid to pull the trigger. A couple of times she shot at one of my sisters' boyfriends. She also shot at B-Baby.

While she stepped out fly and sharp, I went to school and got clowned for the way I dressed and the shoes I wore that were too big. Patty did the best she could to help me feel better. She fixed my hair in the best of styles and lent me her clothes although they were out of season by the time I had the chance to wear them. Patty and my mom were best friends. They clubbed, drank liquor, smoked cigarettes, weed, and chased men, together. The two of them were tight. She and I on the other hand were like oil and water. We didn't mix. Mainly this was because of they way she vehemently controlled my life.

I think my mom was scared that something bad would happen to me. I was the youngest of 11 children. She knew she had one last shot with me, therefore, she hung on for life and squeezed me a little too hard. I think her heart was in the right place, however, she didn't channel it correctly.

Eventually, my mother told me she was the black sheep in her family. Grandma Henrietta hit her in the mouth because she had a speech impediment. Every time she stuttered, my grandma thought she did it on purpose. She told the other siblings to slap her in the mouth when she couldn't get the words out fast enough. Grandma Henrietta would belittle mom when she came to visit her, especially if my mom had been drinking. On the other hand, my Aunt Octavia, the baby girl, was an alcoholic and she was allowed to sleep when she was drunk. Nothing was said or done to her.

One time, my mom moved up north to work as a model. She also worked in a crab factory in Newport News, Virginia. At that time, she only had Danny and Brenda. She sent her checks back home to my grandma. Sometimes, my mom would come back home to visit and she didn't like the way my grandma or someone in the house would refer to her children as "crumb snatchers." My mother's children were the last to eat but it was her money that fed everyone. The pattern was similar to the way my mom treated me and some of her own children. I think my mom chose Patty to be her hang out friend because she did not have a connection with her mom and wasn't that close to her sisters.

My mother's brother, Thomas, saw the unfair treatment my mom received and the two would talk about it. Uncle Thomas told my mom that because of favoritism between the children, when he grew up, he would move away from their mother and never come back. When my uncle was around the age of 16, he moved to New Jersey and never came back until 2015. He has since passed away.

The pain my mother lived through had to be an unspeakable heartbreak in itself. Some of my mother's overburdened parenting skills derived from her childhood because she never wanted any of her girls to experience any type of sexual assault. She was raped at age 14 by a distant cousin and later gave birth to Danny. If that wasn't enough devastation, my grandma tried to force her to marry her rapist until my mother's other brother, James, came to my grandmother's house and stopped the wedding.

One weekend, when my mom came back to Heath Springs to pick up Danny and Brenda, Grandma Henrietta sent Brenda, who was two years old, to visit her other grandmother, Grace, on her dad's side. When my mom went to get her baby, Grace had kidnapped her and left town. We didn't meet Brenda until 26 years later. Brenda went searching for our mother back in the last place she could remember as a child, South Carolina. She found my Aunt Octavia in Kershaw, SC. That experience almost killed my mother.

My mom and my oldest sister led a similar life. They were both molested by family members and when they finally met, they found they had the same taste in fashion, wore the same size shoe, and would by coincidence, buy the same outfit. The bond was still there in spirit although there was almost a three-decade separation. This tragedy took many years for them to heal.

Grace told Brenda that our mom left her in an abandoned field and she found her there. That's the story I got from my oldest sister before she died. I don't blame Brenda because a child will believe what's told to them. The Lord answer prayers because they had the opportunity to make up and forgive one another before they both died.

We upgraded our status at Keyway Apartments off West Boulevard. We now had a four-bedroom apartment and I had my own room. I had all this space I needed to play with my toys and not share a bed with anyone. However, as the darkness fell I would always hear scratching noises at my window and scary shapes seemed to peek through it. Every night I would conveniently find myself asleep between my two big sisters, Lee and Patty.

One night, in a loud drunken voice, I heard my daddy say, "Ole lady, Ole lady, I'm going to kill you.

Ole lady you got me something to eat? Got damn it you hear me!"

At the same time he beat on the walls and broke furniture. I then heard him say he would shoot her or cut her with a knife. My bedroom was next to theirs. In my 10-year-old mind, I knew he would kill my mother and I lay there listening as the tears rolled down my face. I covered my ears with my hands to block out the horror of what I heard.

I mumbled under my breath, "Please don't kill my mama," and every time he yelled or screamed, I jumped with fear. I knew he would make good on his threats because he had shot at her before.

My childhood was full of painful memories. I once wrote an elementary school letter to a classmate. You know, the "I love you, do you love me? Check the box yes or no type letter." My plan was to give it to him the next day, but I made the mistake of dropping it on the bathroom floor and my mama found it. When I got home from school she was waiting with a belt in hand. I ran out the door to the other side of the apartments to the playground. I was swinging on the swing set and 30 minutes later I felt something slash across my legs. She found me. I fell down and she snatched me up by my dress and she continued to cut me with the switch.

After a few steps, she'd say, "I'm going to beat you in the name of Bennie."

She would cut me again with the switch and say, "I'll beat you in the name of Tony."

She was being sarcastic by naming little boys in the neighborhood. I yelled and cried. I was mostly humiliated because she did this in front of everyone. They stared and laughed at me.

"You are too fast. You think you are grown but you need to sit your fast-ass down," she said.

All of this violence going on under one roof, coupled with partying, gambling, drinking, and cursing made me hesitant in love and unsure of myself or what I wanted. My dreams were to grow up to be a creative dancer, gymnast, or nurse. When junior high came along, I was a cheerleader and a good one, too. I could cut flips and dance with the best of them.

At 15, I got my first summer job working for the City of Lancaster dump. I painted the building for the city. I was proud of myself because with the money I received, I could dress like my peers and not get picked on. Boy, was I wrong! I worked all summer long and my mother took all of my money. She also took my social security checks—the ones I didn't know about until I turned 16. I received dependent social security checks from my mom's late husband, Buster. At the time of his death, they were still married and my mom and her children received his death benefits. Buster was listed as my birth dad on my birth certificate.

She said, "Resa, when you get paid, baby, you bring me your checks and I will put them in the bank for you."

"For real, mama? Thank you! I will be able to buy some nice things this year since you couldn't before, ma."

I worked hard and gave my mom every check. The month of August came and I received my last check for the summer. She met me down at the bank on the corner that had a big clock on it. We arrived at the counter to withdraw the rest of my money.

"Ma'am," the bank teller said, "you have $90."

I was puzzled.

"Shouldn't there be more money in this account?"

"No, just the check you just deposited."

My mom stood there and looked at me as if she were a deaf mute. I couldn't believe what I heard. Why would she do this to me? My own mother and my own money. But that wasn't all. She had another gut-buster waiting for me. We walked down the sidewalk headed towards Cato's department store.

"Resa, what 'cha going in there for? Come with me right now."

My heart sank again as we went into the Griffin 88 cent store and straight to the outdated clothing rack in the back of the store. They were out of style and at least five to ten years old. I have no idea how old the shoes were.

I picked through the miserable clothing and tried to put some type of wardrobe together for the upcoming school year. I must have did something right with my clothing selection because I didn't get picked on as much. The next summer, I purposely missed the time to sign up for a job because I was not about to let her take my money again. I chilled for the summer and visited Danny and his family in Charlotte.

"Teresa," a classmate asked, "Why do you always leave class around the beginning of the month all the time?"

I was too embarrassed to tell her I met my sister outside of the classroom to sign my social security check for my mom to take. I made up something to tell her. Later, I realized my mom treated me the way her mom treated her. It was learned behavior. I promised myself I would never treat my children this way.

At age 18, I had my first date. A classmate asked to take me to the movies one Saturday night. I was excited about the date and I rushed home to tell my mom the good news.

"Mama, can I go to the movies this weekend? A boy at school asked me. Please can I go?"

"As long as you do your chores and homework, you can go. You must be back in this house by midnight."

My date, Eddy, went to the same high school as me. We were in the same grade. He was stout and muscular with a full-face beard, funny as heck, talked a lot of trash, but in a good way. He dressed well and drove one of the nicest cars. When Eddy showed up for our date he was a little late. It was 10 p.m. and we had missed about 30 minutes of the movie.

However, I loved his car. He had a white Chevrolet Monte Carlo with spoke rims. It was one of the sharpest cars around. I persuaded Eddy to take me to Janet's house in Carolina Courts, another apartment complex in Lancaster to play cards since he was late for our date.

The time slipped away from me and before I knew it, it was about 11:50 p.m.

I asked my sister Janet and Walter to ride with me to explain to my mom why I was late. I knew mom didn't want to hear any explanation. My mom was at my aunt's apartment, the same complex we lived in. When we got to my Aunt Eartha's apartment, my mom said, "You better be home before I do." Of course young people don't think straight. Somehow I thought we had time to take Janet and Walter back. I was late because I didn't want them to ride along with Eddy since they didn't know him. My mother was furious. When I returned home she started in on me in front of my date.

She said, "You think you are grown? I know you are 18 but you are still not grown. I told you to be in this damn house by 12 o'clock and it's 15 minutes later."

"I know, ma. We took Janet and Walter home. I didn't do anything wrong."

"As, long as you are in my damn house, you will listen to what I say."

Then she asked my date if I could live with him?

He said, "Well, yes, ma'am if you are putting her out. I stay with my cousin, but we will make room for her."

I snapped, "I'm tired of this. I'm leaving!"

My mama slapped me hard and I fell to the floor. I screamed and held my face.

By the time I got up to leave with my date, the homeboy had run out of my house, got into his car, and bounced.

No one else asked for any dates because he told everyone at school what happened. Partially because of my strict upbringing, years later, when I had children, I was too lenient and it caused a ripple effect.

One time though, my mom stood up for me. I ran for Homecoming Queen for Lancaster High School. Mrs. Bell pulled out all the stops. I was sharp as two tacks hung together on a wall. I wore a white sequined dress with gold pinstripes, a gold belt with gold heels to match, and to top it off, one of her furs. That day I felt more beautiful and radiant than Miss America because no one had anything on me. I didn't win the Homecoming Queen title, but I felt like one.

I loved my mother dearly. She failed at some things while raising me, the same way I did with my two adult daughters. I wish she would have talked to me more about the birds and the bees and becoming a woman. I also wish she had trusted me more and not have been as mean towards me. Another time that made me happy was when she surprised me and bought my senior class ring a few years after I graduated to make up for not getting it when I was in school.

The violence between my mother and JT continued between them throughout my childhood and when I became a young adult because he would come over every weekend later when we moved to SC. The fights made me nervous. As I grew into adulthood I took this to be a normal thing in my house. Drinking, loud fights between my parents, and between us siblings, felt like they were supposed to happen everyday. I desensitized to it since it frequently happened.

Still, parts of my dream came true. I became a caregiver or CNA assistant to the nursing team caring for the elderly. I went to Community College in 1985 and it made me feel independent, confident, and powerful. For once, I had control of my life and I knew where I was going. Nothing would stop me from making a good life for myself. I was sure I would not live the life I knew about up until that time.

For years, I asked myself *why would my mother subject herself to the long years of abuse?* She never bothered to tell any of us her rationale for staying with him. Later in life, I repeated some of the same patterns in order to survive. The root cause was learned behavior and low self-esteem. I inherited from her the feeling of not being good enough. I also was immersed in the learned behavior of violence from the repeated threats my father hurled and her refusal to leave him.

As a young adult, I asked her one day, "Why did you allow a child molester to stay in your home around your girls?"

She said, "I regret what I did while I raised y'all. I should have never let him in my house, especially after his wife, Martha, warned me." She said, "Bell, I know you think you are doing something by sleeping with my husband and moving him in your house around all those girls. You are going to regret it when he starts sleeping with them like he did our girls."

My mom ignored Martha because she told me in those

days, women weren't strong and independent as we are now. At the time, she had a lot of small children to feed and her husband, Buster, had run off with another woman across town and left this burden and responsibility to her. She could not handle it and she drank heavily to mask what happened to her and to her girls. That was the explanation my mama gave concerning why she allowed JT to live in her home after her suspicions moved from speculation to undeniable proof. How could any mother stand for something like that and to top it off, keep having sex with him? Bell had some real demons.

The Soul of A Woman

A woman's soul can be characterized by some of the following words: happy, joyful, pure, and sad. But unfortunately someone reading this may have their own words to add to this list. Whatever their list man contain they cannot argue that they all pertain to a woman's soul. A woman with a happy soul is pleasant in all that she encounters in a day, whether it be gossip, jealousy, or strife. It is Jesus' love that dwells inside and shines through to the outside just as the virtuous woman's does. Then there is the joyful and pure soul of a woman so loving, caring, peaceful, and pleasant. Just like the soul of a happy woman they go hand in hand. For some of women who don't know Christ, our soul is filled with all types of sadness because their is no light abiding on the inside. The Holy Ghost talks to our spirit and shows us how to receive and give love. So sisters, mothers, aunts, grandmothers, and daughters, "What's really in your soul of a woman?"

—Dinah Reid

CHAPTER 5

On the Fringes

I thank God for allowing me to witness these events. When I saw family members go through the wild drug binges, it made me say at an early age, "No way, José, not for me." The drug epidemic didn't miss me entirely because I grew up dating drug-addicted men, had one drug-addicted baby daddy, and I married two drug-addicted men.

The first time I felt what I thought was love was in the arms of a married man named Vee. He lived off North Graham street on a street called Grimes. This was ironic because little did I know the name of his street would be the center part of our one-year fling.

At this point, I had only cared deeply for two men. One was Vee and the other one was RW. RW played me from the age of 15 to 22. He lived in Charlotte in Boulevard Homes. He visited me off and on. I broke it off with him when I was 17 because he constantly lied to me. He was involved with a girl he had screwed since she was 14. We hooked up again when I moved to Charlotte in 1985. He was still with the same chick and told the same lies.

One night, he came over to my house. He cried and put his head in my lap. He said he didn't love the girl he was living with and if I married him, he would leave her for good. I knew that was a lie. He couldn't help himself and I had been stupid for a long time, but not that night. We argued and I told him to take his lying self back to the girl he was with and marry her because I was fed up with his lies. He wouldn't leave. I slapped him in the face, scratched his neck, then bit him in the chest. He left only to return about an hour later with his girl. He wanted her to fight me.

I was about to get her but my mom pulled out a gun. "Get the hell off my porch and leave her alone!" she shouted.

To this day I don't know what attracted me to him. He had beautiful white teeth and pretty brown skin. I think his teeth got me. He listened well and married her the next year. One time, his girl came over to my house to tell me I had burned him. I got tested, brought the results back and gave them to her. I was negative. Someone else burned him. It could have been her.

Vee was married but he didn't bother to tell me. I found out six months into our relationship when his wife, who was supposed to be girlfriend, called the house and asked for him. They were separated and she lived in New York with his mother. Check this out. She and I had the same birthday and years later after they finally divorced, our paths crossed again. I went to NY with him and some friends and I met his mother.

She made a point of saying, "You look like my son's ex-wife."

I don't know if that was a shot or what. His ex-wife looked nothing like me, boo. I thought I was in love with Vee. I later learned this was a demonic soul-tie sent straight from the devil.

Years later, he almost got killed messing with someone else's wife. His wife at the time, left him for a cop, and she took him to the cleaners. She took all of his money out of the bank. He ended up on crack and married a mentally unstable woman. One night she stood over his bed with hot tar and was about to pour it on him like when soul singer Al Green's ex-girlfriend poured hot grits on his back while he was in the bathtub. Her attack was thwarted when he awakened. At least that's the story he told me.

With Vee, I confused sex with love. He was older and married and did things to my 22-year-old body that many younger females had already experienced. Breaking it off was temporary. I ran right back to him. We didn't always jump right in the sack. Sometimes we would talk for hours about what I wanted to do with my life. He laughed at my jokes and he was gentle with me. I thought I was the only one until I found out about another woman he was sleeping with. He almost got killed over her. It was hard to end our relationship, but I finally put myself in his wife's place. *How would I feel if my husband did to me what I did to his wife behind her back?*

After reading about the first couple of men in my life, you might wonder if there were any good ones? To my memory, no! Women should not allow liars or cheaters in their lives. I say this with all honesty because I do not want any woman reading about my life as it were, to accept any of it as love. Maybe a couple of men did not verbally or physically beat on me. Yet, they lacked integrity and were liars because they had other girlfriends, women, or wives, when I started with them and I wasn't good enough for either of them to make me first. Stupid me, I was desperate for love and I lowered my standards in hopes of winning them over with sex. This is never the case ... I was an easy sex playmate.

RR was a man with a military background. I knew him from South Carolina. His sister, Cat, got the ball rolling with us during my senior year in high school. RR went to school with my brothers and lived across town from me. He tried to talk to me in school but I turned him down. He was a pretty good guy but I think the distance and timing was off. His sister hooked us up years later after he had moved away from Lancaster.

He was medium built, sweet, and cute as a button. He was raised to respect women and he knew how to treat a woman, too. He lived in Maryland during our courtship, therefore, it was a long-distance relationship. He treated me with much kindness and sent me money to visit him, but the strain of a long-distance love was too much. I found out he had a lover in Maryland after we broke up. I learned of this from his brother, John. He did come back for me after I had my oldest child, Krystal, but out of pride, I did not tell him the truth. When he came back to see me a year later he asked me how Carlton, my daughter's dad treated me? I lied.

Then, there was RC. He was a cool dude who worked as a machinist or welder or something like that. I was introduced to him by my sister, Maryann. RC was a lot of fun. He cracked jokes all the time and had a quirky sense of humor. He would always come by on his way to, or from work, and sometimes I would go over to his house for some grown up action. The only thing wrong with RC was his current situation. He respected me and even took me to meet his family down in a little town called Moncks Corner.

I broke it off with him because he would not make the decision to end his relationship with his church-going girlfriend in Gastonia. RC would come see me every day except Sunday because he spent that day with her. She did not seem like a girlfriend to me because he was with me during the week. I got tired of being in second place. I was okay that he moved on with her. Now, I did not have to make excuses for him or myself for sleeping with him out of convenience, when I was bored, or had nothing planned with no one else.

One evening, he came over to take me to the Hornet's basketball game. When he came over, I had company. He left but called me to put me in check about the other guy.

I asked him, "How are you going to call yourself having an attitude with me and my choices when you have a girlfriend who means the world to you? You would not give her up for me. What I do is my business because it is clear I am not your girl."

He came back about 20 minutes later and we went to the game. We stopped seeing each other after that and I learned from my sister he was about to marry the girl from Gastonia.

RM was a cute and clever dude. He had a beautiful smile that lit up the room and can't miss, cute dimples. I met him one night at a club called Side Effects. He was shooting pool when he spotted me with my "adorable self" as he put it. I was all glammed-up with my dimples and glorious smile. We dated briefly back and forth for a couple of years, before and after, I had Krystal. He worked at UPS and went to school for engineering. He too, came by on his way to work or school. We stopped dating because he asked me not to spend the weekend with Carlton when he came home on leave from the Navy. I ignored him and went anyway since he actually dated a girl named Susan at the time. He sounded like RC.

The following Monday, he called and was pissed off because I did not follow his instructions to not go with Carlton the previous weekend. He dipped out on me out of pride because he did not have the opportunity to score that weekend. Later, he came back around to tell me he was about to get married. I assumed his bride-to-be was Susan, but it was not.

Our paths crossed again and he said he stepped off because he thought the guy from the Navy had more to offer me, like the chance to travel the world. Little did he know the Navy guy and I broke it off shortly afterwards. I tried to call RM but he had changed his number. When I did speak to him some years later, RM said, "You were the total package and my dream. I could have been married to you if only I knew."

This is where I felt he was feeding me some "BS." Years ago he did exactly what he planned to do. One year passed by before he came around to tell me he was about to get married. He never checked back to see me or even fought for me. All of these men were clever little liars but there was something they all had in common: They belonged to somebody else. They were in other relationships when we were an item. I was tired of being someone else's side chick. I had already been through this with RW and it would not happen again.

Before, during, and after some of my marriages, I had many lovers. Some were married, abusive, leeches and whores. Karma visited me because I reaped what I sowed in spades. It started when I ran into Carlton. It was the summer of 1986 when I met him one night at a hole in the wall spot called The Train on Statesville Ave. He convinced me to dance with him. He followed me around and gave me his phone number. Of course I threw it away, only to end up with him about six months later. On January 1, 1987, I left the A&P grocery store and walked down Beatties Ford Road.

I heard someone shout, "Hey, Doris! Doris! Hey, girl, you wait up!"

I continued to walk. I thought, *I don't know who Doris is but she needs to turn around because someone is really trying to stop her.* He ran and caught up to me.

He said, "Hey, you remember me from The Train on Statesville Road?"

I said, "Yeah, I remember. Carlton, right? And by the way, my name ain't no Doris. It's Teresa."

"My bad. Can I walk you home?"

I should have said no, but when you are on the rebound and vulnerable, it's hard to think clearly. It's especially hard when you suffer from the influence of a broken heart. I needed to vent. He was funny, made me laugh all the time, and was as goofy as the dog. I still was not attracted to him but the laughter broke the ice and I let him in. I slept with him quickly. He was slick and played the church role with me. He read the Bible and went to church. He was also a real good false prophet. He could cry and praise God with the best of them.

Three weeks after joking around with him I became pregnant with Krystal. That's when I found out he smoked crack cocaine like most everyone else I knew. I decided to stick it out with him because he was in the navy and I thought that was my ticket out of hell. My plans for my life with Carlton backfired on me because he was heavily into his addiction to crack, tricking off with other women, partying, and drinking.

He turned out to be a crack-addicted whoremonger, who gave me a baby and a STD. He lied about not being married and by the time I found out, I was four months pregnant. I didn't find out about the STD until after she was born. He still slept with his wife, me, and anyone else he could lay with. We never had a real relationship.

When Carlton did come home on leave from the navy, he popped a hole in my dream. During my whole pregnancy we talked on the phone and wrote letters to each other about the way we would spend our life together. Krystal was born on October 21, 1987. He came home to see his daughter and did nothing for her. His sister, Carxine, helped me the most with her. A year later, when she turned one, I had a party for her. I now worked in a plant off Rozzelles Ferry Road making cassette tapes.

I finally got up the strength to move in with Janet for a while. I broke things off with Carlton when I discovered he had been over to Patty's house and they had a drug party the night before. He slept with my play niece, Ladeana, when I was at work and didn't come to pick me up from work that night. God showed up again in my life. It was around midnight and the plant was about to close. Almost everyone was gone. It was dark and I was afraid. Janet and her husband happened to drive down the street and they saw me standing there. They picked me up and they served as the ram in the bush God had set aside for me. They asked, "Where's Carton? I said, "I don't know, but I have a pretty good idea."

He came to pick me up the next day at Janet's house to take me for work and we argued the whole way there. He started to tell me where he was the night before but I yelled at him that he was driving fast and he got a ticket on the way. I changed the subject and told him we would finish this when I got off work that night. I knew he was over to Patty's house at the crack spot. The next day I moved from Janet's house to Lee's house in South Carolina. I was only there for about four or five hours when around noon I looked out my sister's door and Carlton and Patty were there to pick me up.

Carlton was filled with rage. He asked, "Where do you I think you are going with my baby?"

He slapped me hard. I bit my tongue. I was afraid of him. I loaded up our things and went back to Katonah. When I got in the car I noticed $20 had disappeared out of my purse. The only two people around me were Patty and Carlton. I cursed out both of them because I knew one of them had taken it. They both denied it, but I knew better. I was pissed off at Patty for bringing Carlton to Lee's house. Later, that day Vest verified Carlton was at the crack party they had at Patty's house the night before. He also told me that Carlton and Ladeana went off to a hotel together and he was mad because she chose Carlton over him. Betrayed again by family, my own sister didn't care that I had asked her not to allow Carlton to come over to her house if he showed up without me. How could my own flesh and blood do this to me? I reasoned it was the crack.

That's all she focused on because Carlton helped her to get high, too. Patty and I got into a heated argument about the missing money.

She yelled out, "Hell, I don't want your man! Your pussy must be tore up because he wouldn't be asking for mine."

This hit me in my gut with a pain no one could even digest. I yelled back, "You nasty bitch. You probably did because you are always sleeping with somebody's man."

During the course of that argument I learned from Patty's boyfriend that Ladeana slept with my baby daddy, Carlton, my brother Vest, and JT. The three men in my life had betrayed me in the worst way. Ladeana did this because of her own crack addiction. It started when she was 15 years old but now she was 18 years old.

The next day, my sister-in-law, Mekya, and I rode over to Patty's house to confront Ladeana. Mekya was tired and she didn't care for my niece. When I got over there, we fought violently then I headed to my baby daddy's house. I missed him by a couple of hours. He had returned to Norfolk Naval Station in Virginia. The next week, Carlton called me and that ended us. He said if I ever broke up with him he would not take care of our daughter and he kept his promise. He did nothing for our daughter until she was around 17 years old. I received an unexpected bonus in my checking account for $6,000. That represented one year's worth of child support. Carlton had received a lump-sum disability check and they sent the payment to me for back child support. When I called to thank him he disconnected from me, changed his phone number and address, and I did not see him again until about three years later. He spoke but didn't say anything else. Throughout all this pain and suffering I prayed and asked God, "Why are all these things happening to me?" I went to church on a regular but it seemed like God was nowhere to be found

This "pretty little thang," he called, "Reese," did not feel loved or good enough and after he slept with my play niece, our fling melted away the next year as fast as it started. This Reese's cup, melted and darn near disappeared. My outer shell was sweet and naive and all I got was a baby in return. I craved to be loved like most people and the cycle of abuse continued.

Sugar

Many people use sugar in different ways. It can be used to sweeten our drinks, to make desserts, or whatever some of us decide to use it for. Sugar, when it is being poured out of its container is free flowing, much like the Holy ghost. There are no lumps or bumps and nothing to stop the rhythm. Once sugar is spilled it spreads in every direction covering its surface. This is the same way God's Spirit is manifested through our souls, free flowing. When God pours out his Spirit upon us, he covers us from head to toe until a sweet smelling personality takes over our souls and makes us gentle, caring, loving persons.

Sugar can become hard, sticky, and lumpy depending on how it is prepared. If it becomes hard, much like us when we allow our souls to be left open, never using wisdom to protect us, we too become hateful and lumpy individuals. If too much heat is applied to sugar it sticks to its surface and burns. Our attitude is sometimes overheated and burned by the way we let others attach themselves to out spiritual light, with uninviting conversations or mannerism which are good for nothing but cause successful doubt when we listen to them.

Most importantly sugar is sweet and it leaves a good taste in our mouths, just like God's love. We should meditate daily within ourselves to see if our souls are free flowing or lumpy.

—**Dinah Reid**

CHAPTER 6

Are You My Daddy?

At the age of 21, I was young, free, happy and away from a domineering and controlling mother. My dreams were right at my fingertips and I shone brighter than any star in the sky. For once, the world was mine. Living with my oldest brother and his wife was a dream to me. I bought my own clothes, learned my way around the big city of Charlotte, had a job at a local museum, went on dates, and got my hair done at the salon. It was a liberating time for me, but of course, this too was short-lived.

I allowed my mother to come around and steal my little bit of happiness from me. First, it was one weekend a month, then two or three. She told me how hard things were for her back in South Carolina. She talked about her bills, etc., and how she needed help. I peeled off the paper and gave it to her.

A few months later, Vest found a house for us off State St., on Katonah Ave. My mom needed someone to help her. She had me in the palm of her hand. The abuse started immediately. I regretted not listening to my sister-in-law, Reba, when she and I talked one day in the kitchen.

"Teresa, is Bell coming up here taking your money from you?" she asked.

"Yes, she got problems at home and she needs my help with some of her bills."

"Teresa, don't let Bell do you like that. Your mama knows how to take care of herself. She been here 50 plus years. She don't need your money. That's for you."

If only I had listened. I would have had the strength to stand my ground as a woman.

As it were, the streets of Charlotte and the wolves that prowled them, waited for me. I hate to admit it, but I was dumb as a box of rocks. I had a big heart but I could be easily manipulated. I was starved for attention. If a guy showed me the slightest attention, I was his. I had such a low self-image. After all I had been through who could blame me?

One of the first men I met was Bobby. He was slick and drove a white, old school bat mobile, Cadillac, the one with the big fins. I met him while I was on the bus going to class at the downtown community college. For about a week, he rode by every day and tried to talk to me. He had a sexy accent but he wasn't that attractive. I kept ignoring him until one day he saw me as I walked down the street and offered to give me a ride. I hopped in and now he knew where I lived. Every time I looked up, he stopped by. This continued for about a month. He wore me down and finally we started a relationship. I couldn't believe my mother liked him because she didn't like anybody. About five months later, I found out he snorted cocaine and laid up in a hotel with a trick. I dated many guys when I lived on Katonah Ave. They all played me. I was never good enough to be anyone's first. I was always their side-piece or second choice. I was someone they could lay up with when life went bad for them or if they wanted an easy lay.

Parents should teach their children the value of self love. If they don't know how, then ask for help. There is nothing sadder than to see children fall between the cracks because no one would teach them, didn't know themselves, or were too ashamed to ask for help. No one knows everything, but children should never be terrified and intimidated because of their mother or father. The offspring will shut down and never correctly learn the lessons of life. This is exactly what happened to me.

Many people go through life wearing the proverbial rose-colored glasses. It's not wise to always see only the good in everyone. Love people, but learn to set boundaries. I always thought if I were kind and treated people right, they would treat me the same way. After all, isn't that the golden rule? "Do unto others as you would have them do unto you." I also believed if I gave others what they wanted they would love me. I'm sure that's why I worked hard to get my mother's approval, but in my heart I never felt like she loved me. I also felt she hated my real daddy. I believe she resented him because she couldn't get him to do right by her concerning me. She never told me who my birth dad was until I was 15 years old and she got mad because Rita told me, first. The neighborhood children clowned me one day.

Someone said, "That little drunk man who comes over to see your mom on the weekends is not your dad. She lied to you."

I was hurt and I broke down in tears. When I told Rita what was wrong, she told me the whole story. My mom had violated the trust between us like always.

When I asked my mom why she kept that from me all these years when she knew my real dad was alive, she said, "As far as I am concerned, JT is the only daddy you will ever know."

A couple of weeks later, I went to visit Danny in Charlotte NC. I asked him, "Do you know my real daddy?"

He said, "Yes I know him and I know where he lives. Do you want to meet him?"

I said I wanted to meet him. Danny took me to Grandma Bet's house to meet my real daddy. I was nervous and excited. I felt like I was two-years old because after all I had been through, I needed my real dad. He had some things to explain to me. Meeting Robert Jr., was a pure joy. His face lit up when he saw me. He went on to explain how he knew he was my daddy but my mom had someone else and he did not want any trouble. This is when I let him have it.

I said to my daddy, "I don't care how many men my mom had in her life. You are my dad and you should have been there for me."

He looked at me in shame with egg on his face. I spent the night over at Grandma Bet's house with him and the next day he took me shopping and gave me some money.

He and I looked exactly alike from our heads to our feet. After we met, I only saw him three other times. He died when I was 26. I went to his funeral. This blew me away. I had only known of him for ten years. I never got to bond with him because he didn't make the effort to forge a relationship even after I made repeated phone calls to reach out to him. He always had an excuse but, one thing for certain; Robert Jr., never denied me to anyone. I also met my other three brothers, Tiny, Warren, and Brad.

I did learn from my mom a couple of vital lessons: Don't take care of a grown man and pay my own bills because people will let you down and you will wind up on the street. Some of my siblings took advantage of me because I was kind-hearted. They knew I loved them since I looked up to all of them. I was proud of myself that I had moved my mom from South Carolina to North Carolina in order for me to take care of her. *Perhaps things would be different,* I thought. This was not the case.

I came home from school one day and my mom had moved an entire family in our house. Janet and Walter and three children now lived with me and no one asked me anything. Janet said they wanted to move up here with us. Walter needed a job since he lost his job at Springs Mills in Lancaster, SC. Like that, they were jammed in on top of us. Without any explanation from my mom I had to give up my bedroom and sleep with my mom in the other bedroom. We had a two-bedroom house on Katonah and this house had seen it's share of hell.

After my sister and her family moved out about three months later, Patty, her boyfriend, and her four children, and my four older brothers, Danny, Fred, Vest, and B-Baby moved back in. I was the only one who worked. I took care of five drug addicts with the little income I made from the museum and from my job as a waitress at Po'Folks restaurant. My mom received SSI and a Social Security check but I still paid her bills. I cried at school and cried at home when I went to sleep because I was burned out. I came home to a nasty house—cooked, cleaned, babysat, and allowed drug addicts in and out all night long. My siblings slept and ate during the day.

For the most part, my mom laid up in a room asleep with her boyfriend. I had to deal with the crack smoke, needles, and burned up spoons I collected from around the house. I did not tolerate nastiness at all. I would stay up and clean because I knew after midnight they would come, one right after the other, and tap on the door. Fred would help me clean and cook sometimes because he was also a neat person. I believed filth and nastiness got under his skin and blew his high. I was happy for the times he helped me out because I was emotionally exhausted and physically tired. I was sleep deprived and angry. I developed a hatred for my mom because these activities continued for a long time.

Every time I brought up putting them out, she would say, "You keep on living. Those are my children just like you are my child. You are no better than them and you don't know what your children are going to do when they get grown."

That was her explanation for allowing them to run rabid all day and night through our house. I believe she didn't want to live alone and her fear cost me greatly. I desperately looked for a way out of this vicious cycle of being used by a whole family of people who were in it to get whatever they could from me. They were happy like the men in my life who were soul manipulators. They sucked the life right out of me. The rage and wrath built up in me little by little. Every time I had to deal with heartbreak and rejection, the more bitter I became.

My only outlet was the men I was involved with. At least I could escape the events at home for a little while. I sometimes dated a guy named Tim. My sister Patty named him "the funeral home man" because he always had one flower when he came to see me. After about three months he raped me. It was the summer of 85 and no one else was home. I told Tim a few days earlier, I did not want to date him. I didn't want a boyfriend. He wasn't my type and had nothing to offer me. I got out of the shower, and he knocked on the door. I had on a gown, house robe, and panties when I answered.

I don't know why I opened the door that day, but I figured he understood what I told him on the phone about not wanting a relationship. He was cool and never showed me any hint of meanness or violence. I sat on the sofa and he looked at me in a strange sort of way. I didn't think much of it at the time.

He asked, "Why are you doing me like this? Why don't you want to see me anymore?"

I made an effort to explain it to him again. He violently grabbed me and he threatened to punch me in the face. He pinned me down on the sofa, ripped my underwear off, and raped me. I laid there with my hands pinned underneath me while he was on top of me. I cried the entire time.

I said, "You don't have to do this. Please get off me and leave me alone."

He looked at me, pulled up his pants, and said, "I'm sorry."

Then, he left. I beat myself up for being stupid. Although it was what we call "date rape" today, I didn't report it because I felt like part of it was my fault for answering the door not fully dressed. Plus I did date him. When I told Patty about it, she made me feel worse because she said I tempted him to rape me since I was not properly dressed. The guilt and shame damaged me. I blamed myself for the rape and pushed it to the back of my mind. I never saw Tim again until about 12 years later at a church revival. After the program he came to me and apologized again.

He said, "I was messed up back then and sorry for all the lies I told you and for what I did. I'm married now and God has changed my life." I looked at him with shock and disbelief because he dared tried to explain away what he did years earlier.

Seeing him again and hearing what he had to say, did nothing for the scars of shame I wore all those years.

Summer Leaves; Fall Leaves

Think of summer and all of its beautiful splendor. The colors of this season are so visual and full of wonderful bloom. The leaves of summer are rich in dark green color and vibrant in appearance. What comes to mind when we think of the leaves of summer is "life."

Fall leaves are different from the leaves of summer. They are hard, dry, and crumbly in their texture and sound. Dead dry reamains of the summer leaves are what become of the fall leaves. We too, when going through a transformation in life, can become as the summer leaves or the fall leaves.

During our changes in life let us stop and ask ourselves, "Are our souls like the summer leaves full of nourishing life, or dead, decaying remains of something that was once beautiful?"

—**Dinah Reid**

CHAPTER 7

Missing the Target

My first eye-witness account with drug addiction in my family concerned Rita. There were other siblings that fell victim to this drug epidemic. It hit all four of my brothers—Danny, Fred, B-Baby, and Vest, as well as three of my sisters—Rita, Patty, and Brenda. Rita was basically the second matriarch in the family. She took care of us. I went everywhere with Rita and called her "mama" because my mother was preoccupied with my step-dad and her friends. They drank so much on the weekends at the liquor house off Highway 16 and Plank Road that she hardly noticed anything until something bad jumped off.

Rita lived in a housing complex called Piedmont Courts in Charlotte during the early 70s. She was beautiful, smart, and intelligent. She could count huge numbers in her head and might be a penny off. She was funny and could tell the best jokes that made your knees buckle with laughter. She could be sweet as cotton candy sometimes and sharp as a razor the next. Nobody could put you in your place and curse you out like she could.

She also had the best figure of all of the girls and she wore it well. Man, she could put on an outfit and turn heads quickly. Every female wanted to be her in that dress or whatever she chose to put on. She had it going on as people would say. In the fall of 1975, we drove her back home to Charlotte from Lancaster, SC. Jean Potts, Patty's boyfriend, drove the station wagon that we were all cramped in as we traveled down 521 North. Rita constantly said she had to pee. Jean pulled over on the side of the road for her.

She hollered to Patty, "I need it!"

"It" at the time was the needle she used to shoot up her heroin. We drove to my daddy's house and she screamed, shook, and foamed at the mouth. People held her down and gave her Hersey bars and black coffee. I was in shock. This was my second mom. My eyes became open to our family drug heritage. My heart hurt for Rita.

Over the years we talked about our lives. In 1998, she lived with me on Freedom Drive.

I asked her, "Why did you get on drugs?"

She said, "I was heartbroken and damaged when I was 19 years old. I had been married and divorced with five children and no one to help me. I was constantly being beaten up by my alcoholic boyfriend, and our mom did nothing to stop JT from molesting me. To top it off, Danny used to come over to Piedmont Court and use my weakness for heroin as an excuse to sleep with me because he knew I was sick and needed the drug. Being a user of the same drug, he would tell me he would pay my rent and give me some of the drugs if I slept with him. He said I wasn't his real sister... ."

That blew my mind. I thought, *If Danny was still alive, I would have tried to kill his ass like I did when my other brother, Fred, did the same thing to Lee, a few years ago.*

I sat there in shock as the tears rolled down our faces. I might have cried harder than her because I looked up to Danny. We all have skeletons in our closets but I know with everything in my soul that Rita told me the truth.

Then, Rita asked, "Promise me, Resa, that even if I'm dead and gone, you will never do drugs no matter how hard life gets?"

She put an emphasis on crack cocaine. Rita said to me "I managed to kick a 14-year heroin drug habit, but I can't beat crack cocaine addiction. I hate it and I believe it to be the spawn of the devil himself."

We sat at my kitchen table and cried like we were children who had been whipped. Another reason I believe she was telling the truth, happened when I was around 8 or 9. B-Baby, Vest, and I often went to Piedmont Courts to play with my little nieces and nephews.

One day I sat on her steps and Danny and some of his friends came over. Danny and Rita headed to her bedroom. She wore a thick white robe. Some time passed and they came out of her bedroom and Rita went and got into the shower. During that conversation in 1998, I told Rita I remembered the bedroom incident with Danny when she lived in Piedmont Courts and Rita cried even more.

She looked at me and asked, "You remember that?"

I answered "Yes." I asked her if that was one of the times Danny had slept with her?

She said, "Yes."

Years later, it was rumored that Danny was the father of one of her children. I do not blame my sister for what happened to her because none of this was her fault. A lot of it was our mom's fault and two demons named heroin and crack. It's no wonder she got on drugs to self-medicate. She didn't want to feel or face the pain of what happened to her.

The next sibling I personally witnessed with a drug problem was Danny. I visited him, my nephews, and nieces during the summer breaks. One day, I was outside swimming and wanted to go inside to get something to drink. As I turned the corner, I came face to face with Danny who had a belt tied around his arm. A needle dangled from it. Now this one was a real shock to me because he was well-dressed, had lots of money, drove nice cars, had a motorcycle, and would give his family and baby sister whatever they asked. The only time he was mean as the devil was when he was drunk and hung over. When I caught him shooting up, I realized there was more to it.

Another time happened when my youngest daughter was born. I came downstairs to unlock the back door to let him in. I later went down and caught him shooting up by using my mother's coffee mug and heating up the bottom of a spoon with a lighter. This time I stood up to him and cursed him out like a dog. I threw away the mug and told her I broke it.

Then, of course I witnessed B-Baby. About three to four months before he died, he stopped using drugs and said he wanted to change his life. During this sober period I witnessed severe withdrawals. He acted the same way my older sister did that day in the 70s. He was balled up in a fetal position. He sweated, shook, threw up, and cried. My mom went into the kitchen and mixed up some garlic water, onions, etc., and told my brother to drink it. Shortly afterwards he felt better until the next withdrawal.

I wasn't in the middle of drug addiction firsthand, but I wish I could say the same about sexual molestation. After my brother-in-law, the next time I was approached by family members, they were all three first cousins. Two were brothers. Aunt Octavia lived in Kershaw, South Carolina. She had a big family that consisted of 13 children. I loved going down there in the summer time to eat off of her plum tree. A few years later, her son came to live with us. Stan was muscular, funny, and beat the breaks off the best of them, but little did I know he would be after me, too.

He was my big cousin and he was fun to be around. I laughed constantly at his jokes. It was hot on this particular day and I was upstairs cleaning up my brothers' room. This was something I did on the regular because I was like Cinderella in our little roach-infested apartment. Being dirty gave me heebies-jeebies and the roaches were too much. They were everywhere. They swung off the ceiling, crawled around the refrigerator, and sucked food from our outside table that my mom used for an indoor table because she couldn't afford a kitchen table.

Stan walked in and said, "I have something to show you."

I asked, "What are you talking about?"

He asked a second question. "Have you ever had sex?"

I said, "Stan, you are crazy. What are you talking about, cuz?"

He had a porn magazine in his hand and tried to show me some photos. I turned away from him and that's when the attempted rape took place. Stan knocked me down, wrestled me to the bed, and tore my underwear and shorts off and was about to forcibly have sex with me. I screamed, yelled, and hollered for anybody to hear me. Then God intervened and sent Lee to my rescue. Lee hit him with all she had and pulled him off of me. He ran by her and down the stairs. I hated myself because it seemed my looks kept getting me into trouble.

Lee looked me over and asked, "Did he get inside of you?"

I said, "No, but if you had not come to my rescue, he would have raped me. He had tried to put his penis in, but you stopped him before he could go through with it."

My heart was crushed. How could a favorite cousin do this to me? I found out years later from one of his girlfriends in Charlotte and out of the mouth of his own sister, that he used to rape her and make her sleep with him. That is probably why my aunt put him out of her house. I saw him one time in 30 years at a NACA home buying event, then a few years later, he died.

James and Lenny were the other first cousins. James had asked to take me to my senior prom that year. I was excited! I had my dress and was pleased that my cousin wanted to take me to my prom because I trusted him. James was the cutest cousin. He was a football player in the 70s when he was in high school and was popular with the ladies at Lancaster High. James approached me at Carole's house after I went by to get a cup of sugar for my mom. She was his sister. James told me how sexually attractive he was to me and that every time he saw me he wanted to have sex with me. He said he had a good job and he would buy everything I needed for school if I kept it between us. I ran next door to my sister's house and told Patty and Rita what happened. Immediately, Patty and Rita had his butt jacked up. I knew from that moment he would not be taking me to my senior prom, so I did not go. Three other guys had asked to take me before my cousin James volunteered but when they too asked for sex, I did not choose to go with them either.

Years passed and we saw each other sometimes when I visited. We never brought it up. It was like the elephant in the room. Lenny, James' brother, tried to place my hand on his private parts while we watched the TV miniseries, "Roots." I told Janet and my mother about it. Janet tried to hit him with something. He apologized for it and left our house.

I hate this pedophile/molestation demon to the core. He has been in my family way too long. The reason I tell my story is for people to see these demons can live anywhere and hide behind anything they want to. All they need is an opportunity to strike. That sounds like a serpent to me. A demon in the form of a serpent slithered his way around the Garden of Eden and deceived Eve.

Lee got molested by my older brother, Fred, when she was a young teen. He called her his baby and said she was his favorite and used the same reasoning, "We aren't really brother and sister."

I know this to be true as well because when we lived in Pardue Apartments, one day, my sister walked up the sidewalk and cried.

I met her and asked, ``What's wrong with you?"

She said,"Resa, he did it again. After all these years, he tried to rape me."

He got in the bed with me and told me, 'come on monkey like we used to.'"

I asked, "Who are you talking about?"

She said, "Fred did this to me."

Man, this had me cooking with fire. We went to my mom. Lee cried and told my mom what Fred did to her. Mom was kind of twisted. She did not console my sister, love on her, or anything.

She said, "Oh, lord, you can't tell Debra. Please don't tell Debra, it would kill her." *What the fuck you mean don't tell Debra?*

"What are you going to do about Fred doing this mess to Lee, Mama?"

Mama did nothing as usual about it and she said nothing at the time. I waited until I saw him later on that day. He sat at our kitchen table playing Solitaire or something. I snuck up behind him and placed my hands around his neck like I was about to give him a massage and then I began to choke the mess out of him. I tried to dig all of my nails in his neck and I called him a damn nasty dog to try and rape his sister with his sick-ass self.

With every tragedy that took place with the men in my life, I forgave all of them because I know that at some point we have all been victims of some type of hidden dysfunction that never got addressed. My trust in men was broken badly. I would have done anything to get their approval since I didn't have a father to show me what a real man looked like. The one I did have molested my sisters... and my brothers were somewhere off on drug-induced binges. My mom and sisters were too busy chasing behind men and money. No one was there to teach me anything about life. When life came at me, it appeared raw, ugly, and unsatisfying, because the streets taught me not to trust anyone.

The sexual demons that were upon my life kept coming around. It extended from myself to other family members. Other family members slept with each other. This blew my mind and I couldn't fathom the realness of the situation. My sisters being molested by their stepdad and brothers was more than I could believe until my sisters told me their story. I witnessed some of this firsthand. It took me to a dark place when I found out from Lee that her son had a baby by his first cousin. I asked her where were they when this happened? Lee told me they were off in another section of the house and the children were unattended. This ugly demon showed his head again when my grand daughters ages 3, 5, 6 were molested by the baby sitter of Lee's grand daughter, Toria, while my daughter was at work. Who would hurt such beautiful children? Neither my daughter nor I had a way of knowing that the teenager who molested them was a victim herself. I'm sure proper homework and a background check would have exposed this vital information and we would not have allowed her to watch our children.

Turn Your Light On

Turn your light on for it is your spirit. You go to church and serve by singing in the choir, ushering at the door and greeting the guests when they come in. For in doing this did you turn your light on? You read your Bible and pray faithfully along with your fast, but did you turn your light on?

Doing all these things are required to do God's will, but did you still turn your light on? To turn your light on is to serve others, forget about yourself and your daily struggles. Turn your light on by telling others of your testimony, give of your time to help someone in else in need. This is how you turn your light on.

A cooked meal, a ride to the store, an encouraging word to someone, the clothes you gave away or someone else's bill you paid expecting nothing in return. Next time you think about your spirit, ask yourself is my light really turned on.

—Dinah Reid

CHAPTER 8

Motherhood

While I was pregnant, my paths crossed again with S. Miles. I had moved away in 1985 and went back home to visit. She was happy to see me and we talked. She couldn't believe I was pregnant.

I asked her, "Why did you fight me all the time as we grew up?"

At first she didn't answer. She took me to the store and bought me two maternity outfits. Then, kind of out of the blue, she explained her reasons. She said, "One of our neighbors did not like you and could not stand your guts. The neighbor gave me money on a regular basis to bully you and fight you."

I couldn't believe it because the neighbor she spoke of was a distant cousin of mine. Her mother and my mother grew up like sisters in the same house. When I met her, I considered her as my cousin. There it was again, broken trust in the name of family. S. Miles apologized for all the years of abuse and it freed me to forgive her, as well as, helped me to let go of those scars. Plus, I understood Matthew 6:14 which states, "For if you forgive other people when they sin against you, your heavenly Father will also forgive you."

How did I know this? This will sound hypocritical, but it was my mom who first introduced me to God. This is the greatest gift a mother can give to her child and on 422 Katonah Ave., my faith would be tried more times than anyone could care to imagine. My mother constantly allowed the devil to use her because she was not consistent in her walk with God, but I did see her pray a lot and she asked me to read certain Scriptures to her. If none of her other children went to church, she made sure I did. For this reason, the enemy used her to dominate me because the devil was after my anointing. True to John 10:10, he came to steal, kill, and destroy any self-confidence I tried to muster up within myself. The enemy wanted me to develop hate for my mom. I didn't know this when I went through it and I don't think she knew the enemy was using her when she did evil to me. The devil is cunning and crafty, but he can't touch God or outsmart Him.

Most of the wolves in my life enjoyed me as a person until I gave up my body quickly. They showed me nothing except a false appearance of love to get the chance to sleep with me again. Some of them were shady to the point they would go to church and attend Bible study with me to show me and my mom what good men they were. Soon as we were alone, the kissing, touching, rubbing and sex followed. My self-image had been damaged badly. In my mind, sleeping with them was a sure way to get them to stick around. I thought someone would want to settle down, marry me, and ride off into the sunset with me. This was far from the truth. But as a matter of fact, I kept doing it. Sometimes I acted in reverse order. I slept with them first, then learned what they were about. Next, I kicked them to the curve and hoped they would beg me to give them a second chance. I wouldn't but who cared? They had already got what they wanted from me. They would only beg me to stay with them because they wanted more sex, not because they wanted me for me.

My mom treated me badly when she found out I was "with child" as the old folks say. She lit into me because a neighbor asked me if I were pregnant? When I told her, "yes," my mom went off on me and told me, "Keep your mouth closed. People will see it in due time."

Meanwhile I could forget about a nap during the day. My first child and I were exhausted from waking up all hours of the night letting my siblings in, cooking, and cleaning. Every time she saw me trying to sleep or nod off, she would tell me to wake up and move around to keep the baby from being lazy or she would make me walk up the street in the heat to go to the store to buy her cigarettes or snuff. I shifted to sitting on the side of the sofa where she couldn't see me. There was a spot on the floor that popped when someone stepped on it. I woke up when I heard the pop. She finally stopped nagging me after one of her longtime friends, Ms. Margette, stuck up for me. My mama let me have it. She wanted me to make her some coffee or something. Her friend got tired of seeing how she treated me.

She said, "Bell, leave that child alone. The whole time I have been here, you have done nothing but mess with her. You ought to be glad she graduated from high school. She's grown. She's not like the rest of your children who had babies and dropped out of school. Leave her alone, Bell."

Man, was I overjoyed. I could now take naps without fear. I don't know where she got the idea if I slept a lot, the baby would be lazy. When Krystal was born, I became depressed. I was 23 years old and I didn't have the slightest idea what it took to take care of me and now I was a mother and had to figure out how to take care of a baby. I was suppose to finish college, get married, then have a baby. It did not happen in that order and that demolished me. The reality of having a baby to take care of hit me when she was three-weeks old.

One day, I looked at her as she slept and cried hard. I realized at least I could love her the way I wasn't loved and try to make a better life for her. I didn't want her to struggle like I did. I forgot about myself and my dreams. For a long time, I stopped going to school and dove into working to provide a way for us. This took a while to accomplish. I had back surgery when Krystal was four months old. I was scared, and I let my mom have total control of parenting her. After I had Krystal, I received an Aid to Families with Dependent Children (AFDC) check and food stamps. She did me wrong about the aid I received, too. Every month I turned my stamps over to her. I kept about $50 worth to get snacks for my child.

I did the same thing with my check. I wanted to make sure we had somewhere to live and something to eat. Of course, everyone else in the house, took advantage of my big heart. I paid for the house phone and the insurance policies my mom took out on three of my brothers.

She reasoned, "You have to pay because I'm teaching you. When you move out, you will know what to do."

I fell for it. Again, she took full advantage of me. Where was I going with a newborn baby?

The good Lord watched over me even then. He sent Crystal, a coworker friend of mine and JT to support me. If God had not touched the hearts of these two people I do not know what I would have done to survive. They were the only two people who kept Krystal fed and clothed. There were many times I tried to break away from my mom but the hold she had on me was too strong and powerful.

Three years later, mom cashed in the insurance policies I paid for and gave some of the money to Fred. I didn't receive a cent. That same day she went to the grocery store and spent $250 of my food stamps after I asked her to leave me at least $50 for my baby.

When my mother came back from the grocery store she brought back a book that had $5 in it. I asked her why did she spend all of my food stamps? She gave me the nastiest look and did not answer me with one word. I hated her and could not figure out why she disliked me. I thought many bad things in my mind but I repented for my thoughts because I did not want to miss any blessings from God due to hatred. Rita and Danny asked me why I wouldn't move away from her? I thought *where would I go? I certainly would not move out with any of them.*

When the next month came around, I outsmarted her and called social services. I told them to discontinue the food stamps because I didn't need them anymore. Having the stamps discontinued was the best feeling in the world. I felt free and liberated. I was asked what happened and where were the food stamps? I told her I forgot to fill out the monthly report and they cut them off. She looked at me in a crazy manner. She did not have control over me in this area and my heart was happy to see her struggle for some time to feed all of her adult children without any help from me. I don't know why I was afraid of her. Maybe I knew to have respect for my elders. Perhaps I didn't want to displease her.

Despite all of the friction between us, I loved my mom dearly. She could be nice, but most of the time she controlled me. A small part of me welcomed the control because everyone had left home and moved back in. They knew how to survive, but I didn't have a clue. I looked at it like this: I can't make it without her. She needs me and I need her. Being overwhelmed by my living conditions, I let her take care of my daughter. I combed her hair and dressed her, but she would redo her hair and change her clothes to what she wanted her to wear. I let her do this because I fell into a hopeless hole. Day after day, I lived with my drug-head siblings.

Peppermint Blood

With peppermint blood one may think of candy but where is the blood? Peppermint is cool and minty not to mention its sweet refreshing taste. Still one might ask where is the blood?

The peppermint is Jesus's Spirit, calm, cool, and peaceful which is the Holy ghost's core. The white part of the peppermint represents our hurting souls. the stripes in the peppermint represents the blood of the lamb.

Peppermint blood is the candy called Jesus who shed his blood for many. Like the stripes in peppermint candy his Spirit connects with ours never to be forgotten.

—Dinah Reid

CHAPTER 9

Here Comes the Bride

One day my baby, Krystal, played on the floor around the foot of my bed. I noticed she got real quiet. I looked over to see what she was doing and I saw a needle that had apparently fell out Fred's pant pockets. I quickly picked her up to check her out. Thank God it still had the cap on it and she didn't get to it yet. I was mad. I decided I would fix him good. I watched him over the course of the next few days. He hid his needles on top of the door frames, under the bathtub, and in between clothes that were folded in the hallway closet.

I waited until one day when he left the house. I took all of the needles off the syringes I found and placed them back. Late that night, he came back to get them and I heard him talking to himself.

"Damn, what kind of shit is this? Why none of my works don't have the needles on them? I must be tripping or something. But I'm going to find out who messed with my shit."

I was in the room dying of laughter. He paced the floor because he was badly in need of a fix. He left and came back some time later. The next day when things settled down, I went off on him.

I told him, "My baby could have been stuck by one of those needles. I took the needles off of the syringes. If I find anymore, I will throw them away."

We got into a heated argument and I told him to try me again and see. He never hid needles in the house again. Every time I cleaned up, I checked. Fred was a quiet junkie, but Vest was a violent junkie. When he couldn't get his fix, he would rob, steal, fight, or do whatever. I was afraid of him because he could knock anyone out with one punch and had sent many guys to the hospital with his pure strength. He was the Baby Sampson of the family. He would ask family members for money to get high with and if no one gave it to him, he would scream, rant, and rave. He would snatch your purse from you and go through it to see what he could pawn or trade for drugs. If he found money, he hit the jackpot. My mom would give him money straight out if she had it. He bullied it out of everyone else, especially me.

Danny was a cursing and drinking type of junkie. B-Baby was a laid back, jokey kind of junkie. Patty was a sob story-telling junkie, and Rita was a I steal-it-if I-find-it junkie. She would share when she was high. If you caught her at the right time, she would buy you candy or even give you money but you better spend it quickly because she would come back later and wear your nerves down to get it back.

I loved it when B-Baby was high because he was nicer to me. We could actually talk and we got along better when he was high. At least he would go out and work for his high and didn't bother anyone when he wanted it. I knew he was high when he would get philosophical about life and wanted to have long conversations about whatever came to his mind. I was his chosen audience.

Living in such chaos on a daily basis, it's a wonder I didn't lose my mind. About two and a half years later, I was introduced to my baby daughter's daddy, Skipper, by Rita. Rita had five children by Skipper's brother, John. This is how she knew him well.

Rita said, "Come on, Bookie." That's a nickname she sometimes called me. "Drive us down to Camden to John's mother's house. I want you to meet his brother, Skipper. Girl, he got a lot of money. Sis, you got my blood in you. You can get those dollars out of him."

We made it to Camden, SC and I met Skipper. He seemed like a nice guy but I knew right off the bat he was not my cup of tea. The way my life was going, my intentions were to date him a little while and sleep with him for some money. Skipper was a nice person but he was stingy and I couldn't bring myself to marry him. He gave me a beautiful ring and we applied for a marriage certificate in Lancaster County. Then he showed me the land where he would put our furnished double-wide trailer on. Skipper showed me how to drive a standard-shift drive car and would buy me whatever I wanted. He would not put money in my hand though, and that made me feel like a child.

Finally, he came back to see me one night. I told him we were not a match and I could not marry him. I tore up the application for marriage and gave him his ring back and told him to stop coming to see me. I also told him I would let him know when I had his baby. That's why it does not pay to have an ulterior motive when dealing with someone and not being truthful from the start because it will come back on you and you will reap what you sow. I reaped plenty.

I ended up with a beautiful daughter that looks like his twin and about $20,000.00 dollars of unpaid child support. I dropped the child support filing on Skipper because I got tired of missing days from work and tired of him constantly lying about not having a job. I told the child support officials he was an independent truck driver who worked for himself but that didn't help. They still claimed they could not locate him but I find it strange that after I dropped the claim, they miraculously found him and got the $3,000.00 he owed them.

After the birth of my daughter, Korean, I became even more desperate concerning what I would do now that I had two babies and no means to care for them. I went back to school at Rutledge College on Morehead Street in Charlotte. I studied microcomputers and I graduated in January, 1990. I gave birth to Korean in March of that same year. While I was at Rutledge, I ran into Theodore who I formerly worked with at Po'folks. He later became my first husband. Theodore would go to class with me sometimes and he helped me with my computer assignments. He gave me lunch money regularly. He seemed nice enough; why not date him? He was nice all right but he was one of the biggest whores in Charlotte. I still cannot see what his other lovers saw in him. I wasn't attracted to him. Perhaps he was a way out of my mother's house. He was in the Army Reserves and he kept asking me to marry him. I did. What a tragic mistake.

Getting married seemed like the right thing to do. The joke was on me because he ended up living with my mama and I. In order for us to move out, I saved up a paycheck and was creative with the application. My first apartment was at Brown and Glenn, 2121 Custer Street. Custer Street was in a drug-infested area. There were drug dealers and drug users on every corner. I didn't care because it was my first home and it was something I achieved on my own.

I called Theodore a recreational demonic whore because he played games with other women in order to sleep with them. We were married only three weeks and he already had a lover in Columbia, where he visited on a regular basis.

He said he had to go there for Reserve training, but something didn't sit right with me. My spider senses kicked in. I cleaned up the bedroom and as I straightened the closet, a letter fell out of his pocket. It was from his lover. He was a slick one. He had letters going to his mother's address and would go by there to pick them up. Inside of the letter I found her phone number. I called her and she said Theodore was not there. His friend, Jay, called to speak to Theodore because they hung out and talked almost every day. I confronted Jay and I told him I found the letter that was written to Theodore and that I thought he took him around to whore with him. Then Jay told me the truth about the girl in Columbia. I asked Jay to call Theodore on three-way and he told Theodore I knew. After we hung up, Theodore called me with some made up lie. I played along, called Vest's girlfriend, Net, and asked her to drive me down to Columbia to catch him red-handed. However, he was gone.

When I returned home, I confronted him about the letter and we fought violently. I gave him a concussion and he broke my nose. I had him arrested. Out of nine years of marriage came three babies by one of his lovers, at least three cases of the crabs, and a STD. He worked at the Omni and while he was there, he had three lovers who also worked there. Yet, I stayed for more abuse because I didn't want to look like a failure after being married for a few years.

Not only was he a sex addict who cheated on me throughout our nine-year marriage, he was rumored to have dipped in the crack pond. Many of his actions were revealed to me via dream visions.

The Lord showed me another one concerning Theodore. The night before, he stayed out all night. I went to sleep. In the dream, Theodore got a ticket for having sex in the park and the lady he was with, left a pack of cigarettes with lipstick on it in my car.

The next day when he got home, I asked, "Where were you?" He wouldn't tell me. I said, "God showed me you got a ticket in the park after having sex with someone. She also left cigarettes in my car." He basically said I was crazy.

I was about to leave for the grocery store when I saw something between the seats. It turned out to be a pink citation for lewd conduct. There was also a cigarette on the floor board with lipstick on it. I quickly went in the house, showed him what I found, and told him, "God showed me last night."

His mouth fell open. He looked at me with shock and fear. The color drained from his face. He couldn't deny it any longer.

One would think that after all of this, I would have broken free of him for good. Right? That didn't happen until I got into a fight with his live-in girlfriend, Lynn, who had taunted me for months concerning my husband.

Lynn, whom he later married, called me a bitch and said other disrespectful things to me over the phone. One day I had enough. I went to the Intown Suites where they lived. I addressed her regarding her disrespectful mouth. She acted like she had won a prize. In a way she had because when he got with her, he did all the things for her I asked him to do for me as his wife. That pissed me off, royally. When I arrived at the hotel, I knocked on the door and she came to the door and shouted for me to leave.

I called out, "Control your bitch, Theodore, and tell her to stay in her place. The only thing she knows is she is fucking you and she didn't know me to be using such words on me."

I told her she was stupid and that she lived in a hotel room laying up with somebody else's husband. "Know the difference, bitch."

Then, Theodore's girlfriend filled with rage and came at me. She swung and missed. I saw my chance to get her tail for the old and the new, and for coming to my house the week before looking for my husband. I hit her in the face. Theodore jumped between us and she began to whip *his* ass.

A lot of my rage came out while I hit her. I broke a key in half and broke off a miniature screwdriver in her ear. The Lord then showed me it was time to let it go because she could have been dead, and I could have been in prison. Theodore would still be whoring. He was not worth it.

When Theodore and I broke things off after that brutal fight, I wasn't in a relationship for a while. I did date from time to time. The girls were about eight and ten years old when I moved to West Boulevard in the big blue house on Kingston Street. I dated some weird guys. One was a religious nut and the other was a psychopath who ended up on Eyewitness News. He held a woman hostage in her house, beat her, then tied her up and set the apartment on fire with her in there. He left her to die but thank God she was saved. Lastly, came the rapist. Ronnie D was one smooth guy for sure. I met him at work on my lunch break at West Charlotte High School. He was good looking and on top of that, he was an electrician. I never would have thought he would be a rapist, but then, what does a rapist look like?

Ronnie D and I went out for a short while and we talked about his daughter's mom not marrying him. This upset him badly. I was his shoulder to cry on and then one day his sister was murdered in her home in Greer. He was distraught and he cried over the phone. I told him I was sorry to hear that and I asked him to come see me when he got a chance.

A couple of days went by and Ronnie D came by and picked me up. I had on a see-through lightweight, summer dress. We rode around for a while then ended up in a low-budget hotel. We talked and looked at television for a while then later kissed and fooled around. I knew something was wrong with him because he continuously drank beer, one after another. I ignored it. Then, we had sex. The first time was okay but it wasn't anything out of the ordinary. But when it came to the second go around, he wanted anal sex.

I said, "I don't have sex that way."

He didn't listen to me and buried my head in the pillows. He rammed his penis into my rear and ignored my screams for him to stop. I cried and I asked him why did he do that to me?

He said, "Ahhh, you know you liked that. You screamed because you like it."

I knew I was in trouble and I asked him to take me home. I hid this attack and never reported it because I believed it would not be taken seriously because we had consensual sex earlier that same night.

I blacked it out in the back of my mind until I saw him 10 years later at a salon with his wife. While I waited in the salon for Lisa to do my hair, Ronnie D and his wife walked in. I recognized his walk. I sat there and the tears ran down my face. I shook uncontrollably and ran out of the salon. Lisa came out after me and asked me what happened? I asked her if that guy's name was Ronnie D?

She said, "Yes, do you know him?"

I nodded. She said she had known him for years and that his wife was a customer and Ronnie D was now a pastor. I told her the story of what happened 10 years earlier and that I had to leave. I asked her to call me when they left and I would come back.

Later, she consoled me and said she was sorry that he did that to me, but no one could say what a person has or has not done in their past. "You never know when it will catch up with you," she said. Like a runaway locomotive, I jumped from track to track and did not pay attention to all the red flags that said "stop," "slow down," or "caution."

Eventually, Theodore moved most of his things back home and he promised to be a better husband to me and to not cheat on me anymore. He said he was more mature and needed his wife. He did not believe in divorce.

One evening, we planned hot passionate love making and a re-dedication of commitments made between us. Instead, God had other plans for me. We kissed and I closed my eyes. When I opened them, I saw a snake's head. The whole upper portion of his body was that of a snake. I closed my eyes with fear. I opened them again and a flash of the snake head appeared. This time I kicked him hard. He ended up on the floor at the foot of my bed and I screamed.

Rita came upstairs to see what was going on and I told her I saw a snake's head. In the spirit, God showed me not to get entangled with the unfruitful workings of deceitful flesh.

"He is a snake!" I yelled. "Get away from me you snake."

I rolled out of the bed, called his girlfriend, Lynn, and told her to come and get him. Theodore screamed and yelled back at me in a rage and said, "I knew it. Damn it. You set me the fuck up!"

I said to him, "You can call it what the hell you want to but you better go back over there with cha girl."

He then got on the phone with her and she called him a cab and he went back to her house.

Here's another thing that happened while we were married. One of Rita's daughters, Tisha, had it out for me. My niece hated my guts. She tried to destroy me but it never worked. I love my niece and the two of were close at one time, but our relationship changed years later. Tisha lived with me when my daughters were young. For some reason, she told him that I had men in and out of my house and in my marital bed when in fact it was her who live her life like it was Grand Central Station. Tisha slept around and I foolishly covered for her. Her lovers would come by and ask for her. I would lie for her and tell them that she wasn't home when I knew she was upstairs with someone else. In the end, she told my husband a bunch of lies. She felt the need to tell him those falsehoods because I told her she needed to leave my house because of the lies she told her boyfriend. I had allowed her to live in my home rent free for months and every time I asked, "When are you moving out?" she gave me an excuse.

One afternoon, I asked her boyfriend, "When will Tisha move out of my house? She has been with me for some months."

To my surprise he told me he was waiting on her to bring him her half of the money, but every time he planned on it, she told him I took all of her money and she couldn't move out. Soon as she arrived, I asked her boyfriend to express to her what she said to me regarding them getting their own place. He told her what he said about that situation. This made my niece extremely upset. She screamed at me while he repeated what he told me. She became more enraged when I told her she lied about me taking her money and she could have a couple of more weeks in my house but she had to leave.

Her plot against me thickened. She said she would leave but not before she had some words to say to my husband about me. The next day while I was at work,

Theodore came to my job to question me concerning the allegations he received from Tisha. I was livid because he had the nerve to come to my job in the middle of the day and question me when he had only been back in my apartment for a week. We were separated and he was known as the whore of Charlotte.

"First of all, you could have waited until I got home to discuss this with me. Secondly, I am your wife, but it is none of your business what I did when we were separated. You should have more respect for me as your wife to not allow anyone to feed you this BS. You have two choices: Give me my door keys right now, walk away and go back to where you came from, or you can go home and we will talk about it when I get home from work today." He said he would go home and wait for me." When I got there he was at home and we finished the conversation.

One night in the spring of 1991, we moved into our first apartment on Custer Street and had another fight because I had got off the phone with another one of his whores. We fought hard that night. He pulled out a knife on me which he later dropped. Then he drugged me by my legs out the door like in the movies. I went to a neighbor's house and called the police. When they arrived, I could have been killed by them. In my stupidity, I picked up the knife to show the police what he had previously pulled on me. They did not hear my explanation and I did not hear them until the third command to "drop the weapon." By then, one of the policemen had his firearm pointed straight at me and I dropped the knife out of fear.

I thank God for the Holy Ghost and angels who watched over my dumb self, but around year eight, I thought about taking him back. By this time, the girls and I had moved across town in our own apartment. I worked independently. I didn't need him for anything. I wanted my marriage to work for image sake. Everyone I knew who had married in the 80s and 90s were still together. They figured out how to make it work. Why couldn't I make mine work? If I had to do it over again, I would tell any woman if it's not working in the first month, get out of it and move on. Life is too short to be consumed with what others will say about you, especially when your life is at stake.

He showed up at my house a year and a half after the fight we had at the hotel. He said he did not want to sign the divorce papers I sent to him. His whole conversation changed when my new boyfriend, Vincent, came around the corner to shake his hand. He signed the divorce papers without a problem.

Vincent became my second abuser. I married him. My second husband was a loud-mouth brute. He was controlling and verbally abusive. He didn't know how to treat women but was good to children. He walked around most of the time and bragged about how strong he was, how much weight he could lift, and how many skulls he had broken open over the years when he hustled dope back in the day. His demons would soon catch up to him and I found out he was on crack cocaine and he was an out of control drunk.

Although I never did drugs or alcohol, the two demons always followed me around like the plague. I managed to escape one aspect during my childhood but fell right into it in another way. To be clear, I really didn't escape it at all. I still suffered from the side effects that came from living with an abuser of drugs and alcohol. I married Vincent because I thought he was good with my children. He talked to my girls about life and not messing around with little boys and ending up pregnant out of wedlock. He repaired and made bicycles for the neighborhood children. I also liked the way he always made me take the girls and my nieces and nephew with me whenever I went on errands. When he took me out, he would take them with us. He made me feel somewhat secure. I thought I married him for security, but he still ended up being verbally and physically abusive.

I found out later he was raised in a liquor house run by his grandmother. He was used to seeing women being yelled at, hit, disrespected, and controlled by their men. In the environment he was raised in, women were to be seen and not heard and if they spoke when not asked to speak, they were smacked across the face or they received a knot upside their heads.

There were signs along the way when we dated but I ignored them. I was used to loud arguments and drunkenness. I felt he wouldn't hit me because I was good to him. I was a superb cook, excellent housekeeper, and a good lover. I had nothing to worry about because he did not want to lose all of what I had to offer. None of those things matter to an abuser. The main thing with them is control. A woman can be beautiful, faithful, and clean, but if this demon lives inside of a man, a woman cannot change them. She can only remove herself from that type of environment and seek counseling. I did none of these things which is why I repeated the cycle of abuse.

Vincent's size frightened me and when he raised his voice and humiliated me in public, I was afraid to speak up because of his threats. He mastered the art of public shame and got a high out of embarrassing me in front of his friends or when we went out to eat. He drank too much, then got in my face, yelled and flexed his chest muscles to draw attention from anyone who dared to stare. He believed he was my master. If I could have made myself as small as an ant, in order to not be seen, I would have done so quick, fast, and in a hurry.

One time, we entertained some of his friends at home. After Vincent had several drinks, he loud-talked me in front of them. It was humiliating and led to a loud argument. He stuck his finger in my face and called me names. I yelled back at him that night and was prepared for whatever wrath would come because I had enough. I figured when the guests left, he would beat me up. To my surprise, the complete opposite happened.

He said, "I didn't mean any of what I said, but next time, don't say anything. Let me be the man so I can shine and be the king."

I knew Vincent was a narcissistic control freak, a bully, and a loud-mouth brute like those three pitbulls that lived under our kitchen table. Two years after being married to him, I left him and moved out because I got tired of the verbal abuse. He never did anything for me that I couldn't do for myself. I still worked two jobs. I moved back home. After three months, he talked me into coming back.

This was the straw that broke the camel's back. My niece Heather's husband died. We went to Sky's funeral. All afternoon, Vincent drank moonshine. Some people call it white liquor or corn liquor. He became more belligerent with me as we stopped to visit a relative. A nervous feeling came across me. Once I pulled in the driveway at home, he started an argument about the electricity bill and told me I would pay the bill since I was back home. Things would be 50-50. We yelled and screamed at the top of our lungs. I got tired of fussing with him and I grabbed the car door to get out, however, I dropped the car keys between the seats.

Vincent became even louder and shouted, "Give me the keys!"

I said, "I'm not!"

He grabbed me and bit me around my nose. I felt a burning sensation and I cried. I told him to stop and let go. When he did, I swung and hit him in the face. He came back with five blind boys across my face with his fist. He proceeded to choke the breath out of me. I hit the car horn a couple of times, but on the third try, I laid on it.

Krystal ran out of the house, opened the car door and punched him like I had never seen a child do. They continued to fight in the middle of the yard. I made my way out of the car and landed a few punches before I ran in the house. I left my daughter outside fighting my drunken husband.

When I entered the house, Korean said, "Mama look at your face!"

I looked into the bathroom mirror and saw a face I didn't recognize. There were teeth marks around my nose where he tried to bite my nose off. I also had a knot the size of an orange. I was horrified and ran for the first knife I could find in the kitchen drawer. He made his way into the house. I threw some dishes at him and when he came closer to try to stop me, I swung for his face and he blocked it with his forearm. The blade ended up in his arm. Krystal picked up a baseball bat and hit him across the back and shoulders while Korean picked up a machete and swung it towards his chest.

Thankfully she missed. Vincent hollered like a savage and ran into the back bedroom. He came out with an ax. My daughters and I ran next door and left my four-month-old grandson, Kaleb, asleep in his crib. My neighbors would not let him in and they called the police. They arrived and interviewed the neighbors and myself. They told me to go to the hospital because they thought I had a concussion based of the size of the knot on my head. My head hurt and I couldn't think of anything except where could I go with my children? I took some photos of my face to have for court. Vincent was arrested and after they drove off with him, we went back into the house to get my grandson. I packed up three baskets of clothing and three children in the middle of the night. I did not go to the hospital until the next day. I was treated and released.

I relived domestic violence and I placed my daughters in a negative cycle of abuse. It is better to be desperate and alone than desperate with an abuser. I put us in danger. He could have killed all three of us. It would have been my fault. To not have self-love and beat yourself up over repeated failures leads to deeper depression and hopelessness. There was no where to turn but the local battered women's shelter. The good Lord looked out for me. We were in the shelter for three days and the Lord blessed us with an apartment on the west side of Charlotte.

In court, the judge threw the book at Vincent. He got three years probation, community service, anger management, and alcohol rehabilitation. The judge allowed me to stay in the house Vincent had to make the mortgage payments.

I said, "Your honor, this man is too violent for me to stay in the home without him. I will be dead before they serve any trespassing warrant on him. He can have it."

I was glad I got out of there with my life. I willingly gave up my home. Vincent and I had brought a brand new house in 2001 which he still lives in. This was the proudest moment of my life because I accomplished something by getting my girls out of the projects. I gave them something of their own. However, it was too late for Krystal because the year and a half I lived in the projects, the streets got to her and chewed her up. I regret the day I moved to Boulevard Homes with my babies.

I moved there because I had received temporary custody of two of Patty's children. The state gave them to me because my sister was out on the streets and she lived a drug-filled life. I was asked if I would take the children therefore, I did. In the winter of 1998, Patty came to Charlotte to live with me and my children. I expressed to her that I would help her, but her abusive boyfriend could not come. She agreed and then weeks later, she disappeared and left me with two of her children. I had two of my own and I wasn't working and headed for an eviction.

One day, I talked to her caseworker on the phone and I told her I didn't know where my sister was and I could not take care of all of the children. The next day, they picked my niece and nephew up from their school and placed them in Department of Social Services custody (DSS). Mind you, I went to Lancaster a couple of weeks prior to tell her to come and help me out, or to check on her children but she ignored me. She did not show up until they were in custody. This action caused the biggest hell in my life. It proceeded to be one of the largest rips in my heart. Patty held this against me with a vengeance and she went in for the kill. Instead of being grateful that DSS had placed her children with me, she hated me for it and sat out to destroy me by pitting my daughters against one another. Patty and I argued one time and she said she could not stand me and would pay me back at a time I wouldn't expect it and it would be at the expense of losing my own daughters

She and her daughters worked on my baby girl and told her I loved Krystal more and I treated her better. I did not know this was in effect until they came over and asked why I bought Krystal something and not Korean? It was Krystal's birthday and my dad stopped by to give her some money. They made a big thing of it and Korean felt left out.

Korean told me her cousin, Asha, told her I was in the room talking negatively about her to Krystal. She also told her I favored her sister. I did try to have a few private talks with Krystal because she was coming of age and I knew sex would be next. Since Asha had a jealous spirit, I wouldn't let her hear what we talked about and she caused friction between my youngest and I. About a year later, Patty had her children back, but the damage they laid on my youngest was irreversible. Envy manifested itself. Krystal became exposed to a life I didn't have any idea about. I worked two jobs and missed her actions. I neglected her by being too overwhelmed with my work schedule in order to provide for my family. I failed to have regular talks and mommy/daughter dates.

A parent should always make time for their children and check up on them regularly. Make it your business to be nosey. Stay in your child's face. If you become overwhelmed with work, abuse, or whatever, your children will fall between the cracks like both of mine. I blame myself for working the third shift at night, which is probably the worst shifts to work when raising children, especially alone.

To say the least, I was as neglectful as a parent who was on drugs because the results were the same. Krystal's grades dropped. She acted out and had a disrespectful mouth when I asked her to do something. Mostly, she didn't pay me any attention because she watched as I was abused by Vincent. By the time my eyes became open, Krystal had been drinking, smoking cigarettes, marijuana, and having sex all by the age of 13. Krystal also had her first baby at 16 after sleeping with Timmy, Kaleb's daddy. She met Timmy when she lived in a group home for juveniles. The court had Krystal placed in juvenile custody because she was out of control. I couldn't do anything with her.

When hatred is against you on every hand, family will be the first to dig a deeper hole for you to crawl into. Mine wasn't an exception. My family was plagued with lies that started with a rumor. One of my nieces, Tisha, told family members she came by my house one day and Vincent, came to the door with his boxer shorts on and let her in my house. She also said Krystal was in the room with him. The rumor spread more rapidly after Krystal had her son, Kaleb, a few years later. They said maybe he was my husband's baby. Patty, Tisha, and a couple of other nieces started and spread this rumor. I didn't hate them. I knew ignorance and jealousy could be dangerous ingredients when mixed together in a Martini glass of bitterness and malice.

I moved to the Derita area, a neighborhood north of Charlotte, with my family. Mom lived with Patty. I noticed when I saw my mom, she did not look happy. At first, I did not interfere until Patty took advantage of her. Drug user or not, no one will abuse my mother.

One day, my mom had a doctor's appointment and needed someone to ride with her on the special transportation van. I asked Patty to go with her because I couldn't go.

She responded, "My damn head hurts. I'm not going."

I got into my car and met my mom over to the doctor's office. When she exited the van, her clothes were dirty and food stains ran down the front of her dress. After the appointment, I drove her back home and my mom asked me to buy her some cigarettes.

I said, "Mom, it's only the fourth of the month. Why don't you have any money?"

She said she had to give it to my sister for bills. I checked her purse and she did not have a dime. She had recently received two checks, one on the first and one on the third of the month, but she had nothing at all. That did it for me. There was already bad blood between Patty and I. I had nothing to lose. I called in a DSS complaint of elderly abuse. When DSS came to her house to check things out,

Patty knew I was the one who made the report. She called me and yelled at me. She demonized me and told me to come get my mama. When I arrived, it was a mess. My sister shouted how much she hated me and she screamed a curse over my life.

A reverse curse happened to her as she yelled at the top of her lungs, " I hate you bitch! Tomorrow when you have surgery, I hope you die on the motherfucking table."

That stunned me but I had to focus on my surgery. Unfortunately, that was easier said than done. My nephew Steve, Lee's son had molested five of his first cousins and got one of them pregnant. I had to have surgery on my back and at the time Lee was the only one who watched my girls. Before I left, I had a long conversation with Steve.

I told my nephew, "I know what you did to your other cousins. Krystal and Korean are my daughters. I am not on drugs and I am aware of what you did. Now if you touch them anywhere on their bodies or come close to them, I will blow your ass away. Take a good look at my face because I want you to see the face of the one who will kill you. Now try me if you want to."

The next day I had the surgery and when I awakened, my family was by my side. They told me Patty was also there as a patient in ICU. She had passed out sometime during the day or night before and no one knew what was wrong with her. I went in my wheelchair to see her and the first thing that came to mind was what she said to me the day before. *I hope you die on the motherfucking table.*

I returned home to recuperate from back surgery. Before long I felt better physically, but my emotional state continued to slide into an abyss as I tried to stay in a marriage that was verbally and physically abusive.

When I picked my children up, I went over their bodies with a fine-tooth comb and I questioned them repeatedly. Nothing was done to them and my daughters' behaviors—daily school activities, sleeping or eating patterns did not change. I asked them again when they got older and the answers were always the same: "No, Mama, he never messed with us."

CHAPTER 10

No Lessons Learned

When I lived in Boulevard Homes in 1999, my path would cross again with Patty. She lived with me for a short while in order to be around her children after the state awarded me temporary custody. One day she apologized to me in front of Vincent. Patty told Vincent that she lied to him when she told him I was gay and when she said I had slept with JT. She said she was the one who slept with him. And then asked me, "Can you forgive me for sleeping with your daddy?"

I looked at her and said, "I forgive you, but he really wasn't my daddy."

Then in the next breath she said, "He should have bought me the van he recently bought you because I was the one he played all over."

After she said' that, I could only look at her. I couldn't say anything right away. I paused and said, "I knew you were sleeping with him years ago when you used to live in Dillehay Courts because Rita told me she caught you at the hotel with him one night."

Patty's eyes became as big as two cantaloupes and she asked, "Well, did she tell you she used to sleep with him, too?" I did not believe her. She continued, "I wanted to clear my conscience and get it off my heart. Do you think I should tell Mama about it?" She spoke about sleeping with him when she became an adult and knew better later on in her life.

I said, "Hell no! Mama's too old for this now. Are you trying to kill her?" We ended that conversation and moved on to something else.

The abuse demon followed Krystal throughout her relationships. A couple of years later, she had her second son. From the beginning, there was something I never liked about this young man, AJ. He was sneaky and conniving and they moved in together. They fought violently throughout their five-year relationship. One time he got her drunk and hit her across the head with his fist. She had to go to the hospital and get stitches. When I got to the hospital, I asked what happened to cause this and Korean told me she witnessed Krystal and AJ in a fight. I was more than outraged. I wanted to see him. After the hospital staff talked to him and learned the story, the administrators called the police and had him arrested. He later used the phone at jail and told his mother I had him arrested. His mother had a friend she went to school with who worked at DSS. She came out to investigate the situation in an attempt to take my grandchildren into custody and prove Krystal to be an unfit mother. When the social worker came to the apartment to interview us and inspect our home, I knew the boy's mother had called them because she had too much inside information concerning what she said happened in our apartment.

I expressed to the caseworker that I knew who was behind the report and that I would go downtown and press charges on the boy for giving a minor alcohol and he would not get out of jail. Suddenly, the caseworker's demeanor changed and she dropped all findings and left the apartment.

The next day, his mother came to get his belongings and I had a few words for her. I told her and the daughter she had with her, she was a snake in the grass and if she messed with me, her son wouldn't get out of jail any time soon. Some months later, Krystal found out from another girl her boyfriend was seeing that his mom had indeed reported her to DSS. I had told her it was her boyfriend's mom, but at the time she couldn't see it until the other girl in AJ's life came forth with the truth.

Loneliness settled back on my life and as usual, I didn't take the time to learn who I was, or who I wanted to be. I dove into work and filled my house up with family members in order to have some company around. At the same time they used me because I was the only one with an income. I paid the bills and supported my mom who had Alzheimer's.

A few years passed and Krystal was free of AJ. I could not be any happier and relieved. She had focus. I signed her up for Job Corps and I kept Kaleb while she was in school. I sent her away to Job Corps and it was the best decision for her because she finished high school and received a trade. Finally, her life was on track.

A few years earlier, Korean got pregnant at age 16. My world was shattered because both of my girls found their way to early parenthood before they were ready. I worked the third shift again and it proved to be a bad move for me. One night I received a call at work from Krystal who told me Korean left in the middle of the night with her boyfriend. The next morning, I went to Lancaster, picked her up, and threatened the boy again. I left with my daughter. By this time, she was already pregnant and he had poisoned her mind against me. He told her I did not love her and I did not want her to be happy. He had manipulated her with grown man sex play. She thought she was in love and therefore she turned on me.

There were signs of discontentment but I did not recognize them until years later. I asked her why she turned on me and she said she lost respect for me. She explained Krystal had dropped out of school and had a baby without any consequences. She felt like she could do the same. Korean was impacted harder, I think, because her baby's dad, Desmond, was ten years older than her. I went to school with the boy's parents.

At first I was okay when they dated because I thought he was younger, until my niece told me otherwise. I called the young man and told him he was not allowed to date my daughter and I would have him arrested if he did. I didn't know the law.

In North Carolina, the legal age of consent is 16. By the way, at the time of this writing, there are 32 states in the US where the age of consent is 16. There was nothing I could do. I wanted to wring her daddy's neck for not being in her life. Skipper was in her life for about six months when my daughter was around 13. I sent Korean to stay with Skipper a few months before I sent to juvenile detention because of her behavior. It was the same place I had sent Krystal but it did not help. When she lived with Skipper in Monroe, North Carolina, he neglected her by leaving her alone without a phone for 12 to 14 hours while he worked out of town. I could not talk to her until one o'clock the next morning after he got off work because she didn't have a cell phone and he didn't have a house phone. Korean did not get along with his girlfriend. When he and I had a conversation about it, we got into an argument. He said he would not pay two phone bills and if I didn't like it, I could come and get her. The next day, I did. When I got to Monroe and called him for directions to where he lived, another fight happened over the phone.

He said, "You can come and get her and if she died tomorrow, I wouldn't come to the motherfucking funeral. As far as I'm concerned, she is dead to me!"

I blanked out and called him every ungodly name I could think of. He would probably die before her. All of this came about because he did not want to pay child support. When I got to his house the police were there. He and his girlfriend had placed all of my daughter's clothing in the ditch beside the road in front of his house. He had the nerve to take the three pairs of pants he purchased for her out of her belongings.

I tried to get support from the police, but they only said, "Ma'am, get your belongings and leave the premises."

CHAPTER 11

Forgiveness

It took many years for me to let go of the bitterness and hatred I felt for Skipper. I could not believe a "daddy" could say something like that about his own flesh and blood. I had to pray and ask God to remove the anger from my heart in order for Him to forgive me for my wrong doing.

Once I forgave him, years later I talked to him via text messaging. I felt as light as a feather. Forgiveness frees up a person's soul. After being covered by an avalanche of despair, I was ready for some type of relief. Getting into another relationship and marriage should not have been a consideration.

In 2007, one night around ten o'clock, Krystal asked, "Mom, can one of my friends come over for a little while?"

I said, "Yes, but I am tired and going to bed."

Then she said, "Mom stay up with me. Is it all right if he brings his dad?"

"For what? I'm in my PJs and not in the mood to meet anyone."

"Mama, they won't stay long. You remember Man from Boulevard Homes?"

I said, "Yes, he's a sweet boy. How is he doing?"

I agreed to stay up to see him and in blew Reggie, the one who would become my third and final husband. I knew Reggie's son, Man, from years ago. Krystal and he had a big crush on one another. One day Krystal was across town in her old neighborhood of Boulevard Homes. She was with older friends who left her on the path in the woods that led to and from a local store. She was passed out drunk. Man recognized her, picked her up, and took her to his grandmother's house to sober up.

When I met Reggie, I was yet ready to save someone else. The night we met, he was kind and full of life. He liked my poetry and the fact I had a faith-based belief in God. I was a hard worker and he didn't mind that I had children. Our biggest mistake was, although we were both separated from our spouses, we were not divorced. Yet we tried to move on without ending the other two marriages. We talked more than we should have at the time. He was honest with me and told me he was a recovering addict who was clean now.

I told him, "We all have a past. I will not hold that against you. I have been through drug addiction with my family. I don't knock what anybody *did* as long as they handle themselves properly now."

I even told him I was not looking for a relationship. I wanted a friend for company, that's all. He said the same thing. We talked about our failed marriages and I told him I couldn't be with a man who would leave me feeling insecure and didn't take care of his responsibility. He said fidelity was his thing. When he is committed to someone, he puts his all in it. I even gave him a pass. I told him I didn't care what a man's issue was as long as he paid the bills and when he stopped doing that, we had problems. I opened up way too much and I showed him the same vulnerability I showed all of the other men I met in the past. A woman should never tell the new person in her life her weaknesses because a man will often use it against her. It is best to feel him out, listen to him, and watch his actions and don't believe much of anything that comes out of his mouth.

The saga between Korean and Desmond continued. The next two years of our lives were pure hell. I couldn't convince her that he was in fact using her for sex and what he could get out of her. Instead, since she was looking for a way out, she believed his lies. He already had two children by another girl where he lived in Lancaster and other children by several other girls. He didn't pay child support for any of them. When Korean was about six months pregnant, we had a discussion about her going to live with him. She didn't want to hear what I said, therefore in anger, she said something to me that shattered my heart in a billion pieces.

I froze in disbelief. I was in shock. After all I did for her and she hated me badly. Even her boyfriend was shocked.

He said, "Korean, that's your mom. Don't talk to your mom like that."

I couldn't believe he stuck up for me. I went outside to my van and sat there for hours. I cried. I knew there was nothing I could do to save her at that point and I did not care if she left with him. She did.

Korean was love-starved for a man's affection. I knew that feeling well. She would believe anything he put in her head against me. He had a tight grip on her. The poison was venomous. Korean and I ended up in a physical fight when her second daughter was a few months old. I went downstairs to tell her to get the baby and to get off the phone. I don't remember what she said to me exactly but she yelled and it was disrespectful. I had enough. I snatched the phone out of her hand and it appeared as if she wanted to swing back at me and when she got up I threw her to the floor and that's when we ended up in a brawl on the floor.

My niece, Dot, and Reggie called the police to break up the fight. We were both arrested and taken to jail in two separate cars. The pain, disillusion, and heartbreak I went through with her for four years had taken its toll on me. I had enough of her disrespect and now that she was 18 years old, she had to leave my house.

We went downtown and the judge dropped all of my charges and let me go, but he made my daughter stay. A few days later, DSS showed up at my house to investigate the family after the police made the report that minor children were in the house. Plus, Korean had a previous juvenile record of pulling a knife on me.

When the social worker came, the girls were with their daddy in SC. They couldn't get access to them but they came up with a meeting plan to help my daughter with her parenting skills. They lied to her boyfriend and told him if he didn't bring the children back, he would be charged with kidnapping. The trap was set and when he brought them to Charlotte for the parent meeting, they took my grand babies into custody.

That was my second death. I had to fight two years to get them out of the state's custody. I had to do the work in order for my daughter to regain custody of her two daughters. The public defender assigned to my daughter worked with the state in order for my daughter to lose her case. The bulldog in my spirit would not let me rest. My grand babies were molested and physically beaten while they were in DSS custody and we had documented proof. I did the research for my daughter and every time I would give her lawyer the evidence, she would not present in court. However, her lawyer gave the paperwork to DSS to use against her. I saw what the lawyer did and I knew the system would try to steal my grand babies.

The good Lord instructed me to write an email to the governor, city council, senator, and the judge on the case with the information and photos I had that showed what they did to violate my daughter's case. The judge dropped all charges against my daughter and gave her children back — along with housing. The judge said she had no other choice but to return the children to us and they should have never been taken from our home because they weren't in danger and they haven't been abused. She instructed me that if it happened again to contact the Bar Association, especially if I felt my representation was unfair. The instructions given to me by God got her lawyer thrown off her case and her case worker fired.

My message to women is to not feel sorry for a man in his state of hopelessness to the extent you ignore your own well-being. Don't waste your time putting band-aids on a grown man's wounds because if you do, you will be the one left bleeding. If he doesn't have himself together when you meet him, run. You are not his mother, Build-a-Bear, or the Holy Ghost. You cannot fix him. I was a professional fixer of people's lives. I always took care of everyone I came in contact with while I failed to take care of myself.

Something in me always yearned to take care of the less fortunate. I think I developed this mentality because I was bullied all of my life, first by my family, then by friends, and then by men. I wanted to save the world since I could never save myself. Anyone who came along with a story to tell, I thought I could fix them. I only wanted approval in return. Nobody ever recognized me or rewarded me except for my school, but I did not live with the school. I needed something concrete to show me I was loved since I never got love at home.

The Bible tells us to watch and pray because we can be like Eve in the garden of Eden who was enticed by what she heard the devil say, but there wasn't any proof in the pudding. I was gullible, and dupe-able to believe anything at this point, but when you do not know, and haven't been shown the right way to discern someone, you keep getting conned.

As we sat at my kitchen table, we chatted away while we got to know one another. He asked me if I were hungry? We went to get something to eat, and he asked me if I would ever get married again?

I said, "Hell, no. God Himself would have to speak it from the clouds because I did that two times and failed both times."

I fell in love with Reggie because he was the first man in my life who never made me feel cheap or like a low down slut. He made me feel like I mattered and that I was worthy of love and happiness. He said he did not want to be intimate with me right away but wanted to know me. He failed to tell me the truth of the matter of how enslaved he was to his drug demon. I never asked him how long he had struggled with addiction until a year or so after we began to date. If I had asked that in the beginning I would have not dated him.

During the first six months of our relationship, I asked him if he came out of a story book since he was extra nice and loving to me. He was respectful and charming. It was hard not to talk to him all night on the phone. Then, one evening I noticed a change in his behavior. When I picked him up from work, he seemed uptight and snappy. I asked him what was wrong? I figured he had fallen off the wagon and relapsed.

There were signs. At first, money was not an issue. He gave me whatever I wanted and even paid my car payments but I was not aware he had built up resentment towards me for putting him out of my apartment when I felt he had become a little bit too clingy for me. I was irritated that he did not want me to sit downstairs and entertain my family members or laugh, joke, or chill with my two nieces and my daughters.

He had family issues with his brother and had to move out. I rode him around some afternoons to look for somewhere for him to live but we didn't have any luck.

Please understand, I cared for him as a human being and I knew his struggle. I did not want him on the streets or in some drug halfway house. Nurse-mate/ Super Save A Friend, me, came to the rescue again and offered him my place. To his credit, he said he did not feel comfortable moving in with me. When I look back on it now, I should have listened. There was a ton of stress on me. I was the Walking Dead. Physically I was here, but checked out mentally. I was sleep-deprived and edgy. I couldn't focus. I submerged myself in my busy life and took care of everyone and a sick parent. It got to me.

I vented to Reggie about everything. He felt what I said and told me he would help me with the bills. He also said I could quit two of my jobs and stay at home and take care of Mama. This was a big mistake. His drug habit increased as each day went by.

After I pushed him out, I thought maybe there was a glimmer of hope with Vincent and I. We had been separated for two years and he always told me and the family how much he wanted to come back home. I went back to another familiar place of negativity and ended up back in the arms of a crazy man. After we were intimate, he cursed me out like a dog and I left.

On Christmas Day, I got off work and I went over to see Reggie in his hotel room. We talked. He felt betrayed, but I didn't since we were both still legally married. He promised he would not smother me and he would not be insecure. I promised not to cheat on him anymore. I let him come back, mainly because he was not the type to yell and curse me.

However, his drug use became out of control. His pockets kept coming up shorter and shorter. Eventually, he stopped all financial support. He accused me of spending the money he gave me on my girls, although I had my own money. My mom was my client and I got paid to care for her. As the days went by, I did not care what he did or how often he used, as long as he came home every night and stayed away from drug houses. I excused his behavior instead because I did not want to look for a fourth man.

Reggie, like the men before him, was a coping mechanism. He was my daily drug and I needed him even if he were a drug head. We became co-dependents of each other. One hand washed the other. Everybody got what they wanted.

As dysfunctional as we were, I didn't think things could get worse. And again, it started with family. I couldn't believe the lie Patty told my mom. One day, Patti came over to visit Mom and she charged her to shampoo her hair. In the midst of a conversation they had, Patty told Mom I was in the room smoking crack with my boyfriend. I wasn't aware of it until one day Mama cried like someone had beat her. I heard her and went to see what was wrong with her. That's when she told me what Patty said.

I knew my sister hated me but apparently she didn't love her mother. Lying to her could have killed her. I told her I was not on any drugs and nothing like that would ever happen with me. I was on my way out the door to kick her tail but my mom swore me to secrecy.

Then, I had to hide her pain pills because I had an addict in the house with me and two addicts that came to visit on the regular. They would ask for, or steal her pain medicine to trade for drugs. The following year, we moved to another much nicer one-bedroom apartment, off Albermarle Road.

I became a sponge of abuse especially after my mom passed away later that year on December 15, 2008. I grieved her loss badly. I cried and dreamed about her almost every night. I put all my guests out and moved to a one-bedroom apartment with Reggie and Kaleb. Once again I put him out. He came back home the next day and kicked in my door and stole my televisions and the liquor out of my freezer. Finally, he flattened the two rear tires on my automobile. Not it was over, right? Not quite. I took him back yet again.

My life with Reggie was way beyond abnormal. We broke up off and on too many times. I lost count. We got married on July 17, 2009 and four months later, we were in the fight of our lives. Like President Herbert Hoover said about Pearl Harbor, November 3, 2009 was a date which will live in infamy. It pains me to talk about it to this day. Somewhere in Reggie's mind, he imagined I cheated with Vincent because we had ties to a house. He had smoked crack and drank liquor all week but on this day it was more than I ever saw him do.

In the kitchen was a trash can full of beer and liquor bottles which was filled to the top. I knew I had to walk on eggshells, then it started. He brought up Vincent. He got in my face and asked me to go and get my punk ass nephews to help me stop him from fighting me. A year ago, one of my nephews knocked him down and one of his teeth out, for threatening me when I asked him to leave.

Then, in a drunken, coked out rage, he slapped me. He burst my bottom lip and I cracked my foot when I fell. I picked a knife up from the stove and swung it in his direction. He grabbed it and we fell to the floor. I thought he would use it to cut up my face but I only felt fear. I didn't feel any pain. I ran. He took a few steps and fell on the floor. I went next door and called my daughter, followed by a call to the police. I didn't know it, but Reggie was in the middle of a heart attack. He laid on the floor with bleeding hands. The night before, I had prayed to God by any means necessary to stop him and his drug addiction because I could not live like this anymore. I didn't have an idea it would come this quickly or the way it would show up.

The day of the altercation, I did not read the Bible and I was gone most of the day, but a miraculous thing happened. Reggie's blood ended up on the pages of the Bible. The next day, I learned from a friend that he was in ICU. I couldn't believe it. I rushed over to the hospital to see if it were true. His doctors told me to go back and get proof that I was his wife. I returned with the marriage certificate in hand and explained we had a domestic fight.

Things went from bad to worse between his mother and I because she lied to the medical staff and told them he was found all alone in that state and he was not married. This upset his medical team. I asked what happened to my husband because the night before, I thought he was headed to the ER to get his hands stitched up, and then he would be taken to jail. His surgical team explained to me that he had a heart attack from all of the years of drug use and one of his lungs was black as tar.

He was now on an artificial lung. I asked if he had been stabbed in the heart because that is what I was told.

The physician replied, "You didn't do this to him. He should thank you because the fight saved his life. He is a sick man. It's good he got here when he did because he would have probably died in his sleep."

In between working my new job at Charlotte Square Assisted Living in Charlotte and praying to God, I went to visit him like I did many times before. This time he was out of ICU and in a private room. I wanted to discuss reconciliation. I felt guilty that this happened to him and I wanted us to move past this episode. As we talked, my husband turned this whole event around on me and said it was my fault he was in this condition and his mother and brother would get an attorney, sue me, and press charges with the DA's office. I could not believe what I heard. I told him what his surgical team told me and then I asked if he remembered striking me first?

He didn't care about the soft cast on my foot. He explained it away by saying, "But I did not pull a knife on you, though."

I also told him I was at the hospital many times to see him but he was unconscious. "I saw your mother many times on the elevator."

By the time I left the hospital, I was in shambles. I was confused but mostly in disbelief. He assaulted me. He was there because of his health, but he wanted to blame me for all of his shit.

I went out to a club with a niece which is one of the worst things one can do after going through such a tragic event. I talked to a guy and vented about what happened. I gave him my number and he called the next day. We chatted for about a week before I slept with him. I repeated the stupid cycle without knowing why. Afterwards, I told him I would not sleep with him anymore. It wasn't right and I did not want a relationship or anything with him. He understood and said if I ever changed my mind to find him.

I went back to our apartment and packed my things. The plan was for me to move in with my daughter. When I picked up my Bible, I noticed Reggie's blood on the pages. God put it in my spirit not to worry about my husband in the hospital because he allowed the death angel to pass over him like he did in Egypt in biblical times. When death came to visit, he spared his chosen tribe. God gave my husband a brand new heart. They went into his chest cavity four times in the two months he was in the hospital and they replaced five stents around his heart wall.

Three months later, I got a call from my husband. Now, he wanted to talk about us. I met with Reggie in the parking lot of Bi-lo Grocery Store. He apologized and asked me to be honest concerning whether or not I was seeing anyone else. I said no, but I explained I had stepped out one time while he was in the hospital because he turned against me with his mother. He said he did not care. He forgave me, he said, because he placed me in that position. He said, "No man would get his wife."

I believed him but it was a gigantic mistake and a massive lie on his part. We reconnected and joined forces to come together in faith and love, but it proved to be an extensive fight. He spent the next several years reminding me of how I cheated on him. Once more, I allowed myself to live an egg shell life of in and out, back and forth break ups. I divorced him in 2013, but I stayed in a relationship with him.

We moved around to different family members' houses. After that, my family turned on me because I would not leave Reggie alone. Reggie and I ended up living in a hotel room for two years. We moved to Virginia in 2016, remarried, and started our life over. We still have our challenges like others do, but I can say by the grace of God Almighty, He has worked out all the troubles in my mind concerning what being a committed spouse looks like. I never slowed down long enough to learn what fidelity *really* meant.

I said before, "God takes care of His chosen people." Reggie got a job at Lake Region, a medical facility that makes heart stents, the same object God placed in him to save his life. He now makes them with his own hands in his position as machine operator. I got a job at the hospital working on the cardiac floor as a nursing assistant.

I finally figured out that each marriage has its own battles. Some are tougher and harder than others but the biggest lesson I learned was to understand what you can deal with. I learned not to waste time venting to other people about your marital problems unless you are ready for change. I also stopped comparing my marriage to others who *seem* to not have any problems.

Listen, there is nothing wrong if you must seek counseling or talk with a professional to help you with your own personal baggage. When I talked to my doctor and Employment Assistance Program counselor, it was the best decision I ever made for me because I was prescribed the right medication to help with my depression. My rage and outbursts are under control and I know how to think rationally instead of acting out on impulse.

Now, I like myself much more. I even love myself more and I know there is a light at the end of the tunnel. I'm more focused and I sleep better at night. Through all of the dysfunction I suffered all of my life, the depression demon was the root cause of many of my problems. A great number of people suffer from depression and are unaware of its pull and power. They go along and suffer in silence like I did for years and then they reach the point of suicidal thoughts. I lost interest in everything.

What does the face of depression look like? Does it smile? Will it work? Does it get married? Will it have children? Does it have a successful career? The answer to all of these questions is "yes."

Once you know you have anxiety and depression, get professional help. Don't get your advice from television talk shows and beauty shops. I reached out and I'm not ashamed. This is why I wrote this story. Through the grace of Almighty God, I have depression covered under the blood of Jesus and depression no longer has me.

CHAPTER 12

Three Gifts

The best three gifts ,God the Father gave me was His son, Jesus Christ, and my daughters, Krystal and Korean. They both have blessed me with eight wonderful grandchildren to share in this journey of my life. I remember going to church at the age of two and I give my mama credit for telling me about the Lord at such a tender age. From the time I entered this life in December 1963, there were many enemies attached to my bloodline. I hated the sins which the bloodline produced but not the people who were affected by them. These demons plagued four generations of my family and in telling my story, I intend to stop it before my grandchildren can come of age. Each of us come into this world not knowing that an unseen predestined adversary named Lucifer causes sin to run rabid in our lives before any of us were created. Revelation 12:7-17 explains what I am talking about.

> And there was war in heaven: Michael and his angels fought against the dragon; and the dragon fought and his angels,
> And prevailed not; neither was their place found any more in heaven.

And the great dragon was cast out, that old serpent, called the Devil, and Satan, which deceiveth the whole world: he was cast out into the earth, and his angels were cast out with him.

And I heard a loud voice saying in heaven, Now is come salvation, and strength, and the kingdom of our God, and the power of his Christ: for the accuser of our brethren is cast down, which accused them before our God day and night.

And they overcame him by the blood of the Lamb, and by the word of their testimony; and they loved not their lives unto the death.

Therefore rejoice, ye heavens, and ye that dwell in them. Woe to the inhabiters of the earth and of the sea! for the devil is come down unto you, having great wrath, because he knoweth that he hath but a short time.

And when the dragon saw that he was cast unto the earth, he persecuted the woman which brought forth the man child.

And to the woman were given two wings of a great eagle, that she might fly into the wilderness, into her place, where she is nourished for a time, and times, and half a time, from the face of the serpent.

And the serpent cast out of his mouth water as a flood after the woman, that he might cause her to be carried away of the flood.

And the earth helped the woman, and the earth opened her mouth, and swallowed up the flood which the dragon cast out of his mouth.

And the dragon was wroth with the woman, and went to make war with the remnant of her seed, which keep the commandments of God, and have the testimony of Jesus Christ.

When other family members came to visit us, the adults put us all in the same room. That was the opportune time for us to act like we were grown on a regular basis while the real grown folk played music and drank alcohol. That was a bad idea when I was a child, and it is an even greater mistake for parents to do it today. Although times have always been evil, today, times have become even more wicked and twisted. If you put your children in a room somewhere, nowadays you better sit within eyeview.

Here's something else I learned the hard way. Don't be too quick to allow your children to spend the night with other children. Other people's children may ruin your children, especially if their parents don't have the same values. It is almost always better to learn who the parents or guardians are and let them come over to your house in order for you to supervise what they are doing. Of course when they are at your house, their parents may have the same concerns. Therefore, you must be the one with exceptional morals and values. Like they say, "It takes a village to raise a child."

By the time I figured that out, I had lost Krystal to the streets and Korean would soon follow. Being a single mother at any age is hard and overwhelming. And the stress can be overwhelming. I'm not making excuses but this is one of the reasons some mothers kill their children. The world has become cold, uncaring, and provoked by fear and selfishness. We need to find a way to get back to helping parents raise their children. Single parents especially need guidance. There should be a system in place for young mothers to receive a break from their children, especially when they feel burned out or emotionally distressed.

As a young mother I often thought, if *I could get a few hours to myself, I could recharge.* That would have been a godsend for me. If a single mother doesn't have a family support system to help with her children, it would be good to be able to reach out to a non-profit organization or a local church for assistance in time of stress.

Many times I felt like the dry places in my life would remain forever. For a long time I didn't have enough and when I did advance a little, some event would stop it. The one thing that helped me the most through this "ball of confusion" as the Temptations put it, was my perseverance to always fight and find a way to believe in myself. I learned that I am my best advocate. I cannot give up on me because if I do that, then it's over. God has always put gifts in us to create wealth but when you don't know how to exercise them, it's the same as not having them.

I started a poetry line called Insightful Pleasures, an organization called Sleeping Peaceful, and a sitter service called Gimmee A Break. They have not been as successful as I would like for them to be. I listed them to show that I have a creative mind that is full of ideas. Sometimes, one must dig deep to find something that will make you want to live to fight another day. I am a fighter. I have always believed that one day this desert will end. Sharing my story in order to help others triumph over their adversities is a victory for me.

You may be under a generational curse but it doesn't have to be a constant in anybody's life. Proper help is available through education and by knowing the signs of physical and sexual abuse. I hate the sexual molestation demon with everything within me. I never thought it would pass down to my grand babies. When it did, it was the most hurtful thing I had ever been through. We pressed charges but they were later dropped for lack of evidence. Their abuser was smart enough not to leave any physical evidence. She used her mouth to lick on them. My granddaughters knew it wasn't right. They told us what happened. Pedophiles and molesters are bullies who target the ones they consider to be weak. They prey on them.

Through these wilderness times, I had to fully rely on God Almighty to guide me through each process of my life. The system may be broken, but my trust in God is solid. God is always faithful in His promises to us no matter how dark life seems. God brought me through.

He delivered me again and again. That's why I will never laugh at the Hebrew children as they made their exodus from slavery to the Promised Land. They turned their back on God, they murmured and complained, and they worshipped idols. God never left them. From 2012 to 2015, my life spiraled out of control but the Lord was with me.

CHAPTER 13

Family Matters

Over the years, I learned how to pick and choose my female associates more carefully and I learned all women aren't nasty in the way they treat people. It was a valuable lesson when I understood that everyone will not have a heart like, or see things the way I see them. Everyone's perception is different. I wasted time saying *if it were me I would not do this or that*. However, I looked at things from a nurturing aspect of saving others who in return would not, or could not save me. Krystal's wisdom taught me this fact after she came from Job Corp. It never dawned on me that people wouldn't give as I had given or love as I loved. People with big hearts, who unselfishly give much of themselves must protect their hearts and place boundaries around it. If they don't, the users won't either.

The more I gave of myself, the more the users and manipulators took from me without remorse. Family hurt is the worst kind of pain because they should believe in you when no one else will. Family should be your "ride or die" buddies. The fragments of my family dynamic was anything but trust. The pain and dysfunction in my family had us at war. We pulled each other down and hung around deceitful individuals or high-minded ones who had made it to the top and then snubbed their noses at the ones still on the bottom.

Some of my family members had no remorse or limits. They would try to destroy you and Tisha was no exception. Another time, she reported a lie to my next door neighbor Lena, that I said she was a nasty heifer and a trifling bitch to live the way she does. She was not a good housekeeper. Tisha told Lena this lie on me because she wanted my neighbor to fight me. That same afternoon Lynn questioned me about what my niece Tisha told her.

I said to Lena, "Girl, if you are a nasty housekeeper then you are and there's nothing written in stone that you was going to do anything to me."

Lena was beyond pissed when I told her this but she knew it was the truth. Lena said a few more curse words then stormed out of my apartment. Tisha's plan backfired on her because Lena and I remained friends and did not fight. Also her plan backfired to break me Theodore up because we had recently reconciled. When I put her out, she told Theodore that I was laying up in my apartment having sex with a lot of men when we were separated. In fact, I covered up for Tisha. She had different men in my apartment that she tricked for money. Tisha thought by telling Theodore he would leave me again, but he did not. I believe a part of him believed what she told him which explains why he came to my job to question me.

Her volcanic behavior continued into the next week when she orchestrated another plan against me in an attempt to turn her sister Pat against me as well.

Pat fell for the lie she told her. I had called Pat earlier in the day to ask her when she was going to pay me back the food stamps I had lent to her a few weeks prior. When I called Pat to ask her about it, Tisha answered the phone and wanted to know what I wanted with Pat. I told her why I was calling and then Tisha said Pat was asleep. I told her to tell her I called and I would talk to her later.

That night around eleven o'clock my phone rang. I answered and Pat started right off. She yelled and called me names. She said I did not have to call her home all day asking about no damn food stamps. She hung the phone up in my ear before I could explain to Pat that Tisha had lied to her. I pulled my daughters out the bed and drove around the corner to her house to explain because we had never had any disagreements. I knocked on Pat's door and was invited in. A heated argument occurred between us. The next thing I know, we had a serious fight and the police were called by someone in the house. They came and got each side of the story and informed us that we could place assault complaints out on one another. When the police left, Tisha convinced Pat to go to downtown Charlotte and take out an assault charge on me. Tisha's efforts once again blew up in her face because when I went to court to explain to the judge, he dismissed all the charges against me. One would think I would be through with her but I was not, mainly because I love hard. I also never wanted my family to suffer. I didn't learn until much later in life that you sometimes have to separate yourself from people who deliberately try to sabotage you.

The worst thing she did to me was to spread the rumor years later after I was married to Vincent, to say he molested my daughter Krystal. Tisha claimed she caught them in bed together one day when she stopped by my apartment when I was at work only to come back a few months later to ask me if her daughters could stay with me for a while until she got a place for them. I said "no" because she did many malicious things to me. If Vincent did molest my daughter, why would she want her daughters in the same environment? The expression on her face revealed a great Kodak moment. To say she was stunned did not come close to describing her response.

Years later, I welcomed her back into my home and again she didn't let me down. In general, her character never changed. She still spit venom about me behind my back. This time I did not confront her regarding the lies. I put her out and she never came to live with me again. I've learned to love her from a distance. There were other family members who plotted against me and my sister Patty passed with flying colors.

Patty and I were close when we were children. She was a playful, beautiful black stallion, with the best figure I had ever seen. She reminded me of a Barbie doll with an hour glass figure. She could also out dress anyone. I enjoyed the way she fixed my hair in all the latest pretty styles. When I was in the eight-grade, she made my cheerleader outfit. As we got older, our lives began to separate due to her drug addiction. I don't hold anger and bitterness against her anymore, because I grew to understand that I had to live freely to become a better person. The effects of addiction will destroy lives and it does not care where you live or what you have or what kind of heart you possess. This demon is a product of its father, the devil.

I loved my sister. This process of loving my sister did not happen overnight. It took many years and many tears to process. People will misinterpret what you do for them and make you out to be the worst person in the world once you become aware of how they use you. My intentions for my family were always pure, born out of selfless kindness. Jealously always reared its head. That is why I'm glad that I can trust my Lord and savior, Jesus Christ. The word of God says man will see you for your outward appearance but God looks at your heart (1 Samuel 16:7 KJV). I'm glad to have an incredible relationship with the Lord Jesus Christ because He sees me for who I am and He loves the best part of me. After all the pain and the years that followed, God still takes care of me. I didn't wait long for His blessings to take place in my life because I never gave up on Him. Galatians 6:9 states, "And let us not be weary in well doing: for in due season we shall reap, if we faint not."

The question becomes, "How do we love?" To get the answer we should pray to God and ask Him to show us how to love. You will never align yourself to receive the good things in life if you do not keep a stable relationship with God.

Once I took my eyes off of the pain many others had inflicted upon my life, I had to pray earnestly for God to show me how to forgive people from my past. I did not know how to forgive. I was filled with rage, anxiety, and hatred. I allowed these demons to fester inside me and they kept me from being productive with the gifts He had placed inside of me to give back to the world. The hardest thing for me to do was to let go of past hurts. They had been part of me for a long time. I was comfortable with holding onto them. I was raised to not let anybody strong arm me. I did what I had to do to get even.

Thinking like this held me back and kept me at a distance from the ones who had wronged me. It also kept me from developing new relationships which could have helped me achieve more in my life. I could never understand how some of us could go through challenging times and the others who were successfully living their best lives, did not help the less fortunate do better. It also hurt my heart to know that most of my siblings would fall prey to alcohol and drug addiction. Although I was not a partaker, it did not hurt me any less to see them out on the streets of Charlotte as they risked their lives for the next high. I got sucked into the pain a by-product of their addiction. I dated and married drug-addicted men who would manipulate and use me because I cared for them. I had blinders on and did not know how to choose a productive mate. Addiction affects everyone. especially the ones who don't actually indulge. The mental strain and guilt can be tremendous. My mother had eight children to fall to this sickness and one of my aunts, Easter must have had at least ten who did. My mother's youngest sister Octavia must had several children to do the same. Many of my cousins and a few of my nieces and nephews developed a drug addiction. For us, this was our reality. Some relatives hid problems from their family and would not tell the truth hidden behind the ugliness of this disease. Two nieces wanted to know things about their dads and they asked me to tell them what I knew of them. Saturn, one of my nieces asked, "Aunt Teresa what is wrong with our family? Why do they have so many secrets? Do you know anything about my dad, Danny?" I answered, "Yes." She asked me some things about him and a rumor she heard about her dad and Rita.

I told my niece I knew many things about her dad but some things I wouldn't disclose. Then she asked, "Do my mother know?" I said, "Yes, this is probably a conversation you should have with her. My niece continued to press me for the truth about our family but I was adamant. "I know a lot of things for sure, but I would not tell her any of it and I doubt if her mother would tell her anything either." I was asked the same question from Macy, my other niece about her dad, Fred, and I gave her the same answer. If either of my nieces read my book, some of their questions will be answered. At the time I didn't tell them what I knew because I did not think they could handle the truth that both of their dads were molesters and pedophiles. Lee told me about a time when babysat Danny's children until our brother Danny wanted to have sex with her and tried to kiss her in the mouth. She told our sister-in-law, Rudy about it and after that, she could no longer watching her nephews and niece. That job went to Patty. This demon affected Patty in the worse way. She would sleep with anyone's man including Krystal's dad and other sisters' husbands if she could get away with it.

She told me that Carlton kept asking her for sex. I believed she slept with him anyway because of her history even though she said she did not. She later admitted to having sex with JT when she got older. Patty was caught having sex with Janet's husband about a week after she passed away. Her boyfriend Carter who is the father to one of her children came over to my mom's house to tell that he followed Patty to my sister's house and saw her in the bed through the window having sex with her brother-in-law. Another time when Lee and Patty argued, Lee blurted out, "You Hoe! I can't even find a boyfriend down here in Lancaster because every time I do, they have slept with you."

Promiscuity took hold of my sister and I hated what the addiction made her. I believe none of this would have happened if she had not of been molested by my step-dad, raped at 11 years old, and hung around in bars with my mom at age 13. Older males took full advantage of her. I remember I must have been nine years old, her boyfriend came to our home on MacArthur Avenue to talk to my mom about why he was seeing my sister.

A close friend of my mom's told mom one morning as she was driving pass the gas station that shesaw Patty many times hanging out at the gas station up the street when Patty should have been in school. This is why my mom had him to come and talk to her about why he was seeing Patty and if he knew how old she was? Jean looked to be around 30. My mom told him how old she was and he pretended like he thought she was 18 because of her looks. He said he had a daughter the same age.

"I'm sorry, but I'm in love with her. We have been seeing each other for a year."

I stood there in disbelief because my mom said nothing to him about pressing charges or anything at all. She excused their behavior by saying if she did anything about it, the two of them sneak around and continue to date. I would not have stood for it. And if the rumor about my daughter Krystal and my ex- husband, Vincent, ever becomes a reality he will be thrown so far under Mecklenburg County jail system he would die in there, if I did not kill him first. When this rumor started I worked a great deal and as soon as I learned about it, I repeatedly questioned the both of them over the course of our nine year marriage. The answer was always "no." I trust what the both of them had to say about the rumor Tisha started because I know my daughter would have told me. Vincent may have been a verbally aggressive brute that did not know how to treat his wife but he was not a child molester. Everybody has family secrets but they don't realize the impact the secrets can cause on the family.

My cousins had things about them that they hid about their mother but they put things on blast about their relatives. This is the reason I am not close to many of my cousins in Kershaw, South Carolina. There is too much favoritism and puts downs by them towards "the have nots." My mother to her credit did vent to me sometimes about it when it was on her mind. She told me of this time when she dated Fred's dad, Massey. She caught her sister, Octavia and Massey having sex. The shock of getting caught was on my aunt's face but she blurted out, "Well, I thought that ya'll had broke up. Bell you don't want him no more do you?"

My mom told me she didn't do anything about what happened to her but she did stop seeing him. She also told me her sister beat the living hell out of one of her daughters because she caught or suspected her of sleeping with one of her boyfriends. The beating was so severe my aunt almost caused my cousin to lose her baby. To my mom's credit, I many years later at one of our family reunions in the 80s, some of my cousins tried to humiliated my mother by asking her to "Tell us how it was back in your time? How did you all do things?" That historical inquiry eventually changed to, "We heard mama took your man!" My mom defended herself and said, "Octavia, your mom has never been qualified to take anything from me that I didn't want taken. Shit, I gave him to her."

Man, I was proud of my mom for that one. She told them and the look on their faces was another Kodak moment for me. Their mouths hung open to the point, one thousand flies could have flown into their mouths. One of their sister was married to a homosexual and one of their brother molesting two of their sisters. This is only some of the examples of my distorted family. My aunt Octavia's children had a way of saying really condescending comments to my mom and us. But when they were called out they would play it down by saying, "We were playing," or "You all took it the wrong way." When they came for me with that little slip of the lip they knew I would come back at them unapologetically blazed them and put them in their place.

Until this day, they tread lightly with me because they know if they come for me, my mom, or any of my family, once I caught wind of it, I would tell them how I felt about it or what they could do with their information The only reason I'm making some of their family dynamics relevant is because some of them have spent too much time trying to putting us down because we were the so needy branch of the family. They still only deal with a few of my mom's family, "the haves," the ones who went to school and made something of their lives and grew to have a little money. In 2004, my mom and I were invited by my cousin May to one of their cookouts. I felt uncomfortable in the first place because we did not brought anything to put on the table at their social. When we arrived, instead of "I'm glad to see you, cousin, it's been a long time," I was met with the "Who told you to come?"

That should have been a red flag. I should have got up and left but I did not. When we finally got ready to leave, one of my cousins gave me a bag of clothing for my girls that her daughter had outgrown. I thought it was a loving gesture from family in Kershaw SC.

On the way back to Charlotte, Krystal said, "I don't want to wear any of the those clothes."

I asked, "Why?" and she told me "I overheard them talking about how needy we were and how we just love those hand me downs."

I was angry because my children and I are not charity cases for them to feel sorry about. I asked my daughter to describe how she felt and she said that it hurt her feelings. As soon as I walked in the door I was on the phone chewing one of them a new one.

"Do not ever offer me and my children a damn thing. The stuff you gave us would be going to the dumpster." She hesitated and tried to clean it up. She said Krystal misunderstood what she said because she didn't mean it that way. My other cousin kept my grandson's baby shower invitations in her pocketbook for a month and never gave any of them out. Favoritism among family members is the reason my mom and her youngest brother, Thomas, moved away when they grew up. There have been many scars from this side of my family and that explains why "I don't fool with them too fast." God is still working on me in the mouth department and I can only pray that they are working on why they treat people whom they think are less fortunate than them the way they do.

Family should never treat family this way. I broke this favoritism chain off of my daughters' necks. I never raised them to think they are better than anyone else. My daughters had love and a pure heart until I let other people around them who were filled with envy towards me. They got to Korean and started this lying demon to manifest itself between my daughters. They targeted my youngest because she was more vulnerable and impressionable and did not know better. I thank God for Jesus that with prayer he repaired some of the damage that transpired when I couldn't be there. There were many sleepless nights before God healed, delivered, and heard my cry for peace to be restored in my home. Other people or their children can ruin your children. Don't be too quick to send them off to stay over other people houses unless you have spent time with them and learned that family's social environment. I give much credit to Debra because she never let that happen. Her children stayed with her.

CHAPTER 14

The Healing

One month I lost everything I thought was dear to me; my job, my apartment, my furniture, my car, and my marriage. Before this happened, God told me at a marriage conference in October 2012, He would repair everything that the cankerworm stole from me. He said, "Walk in a season of expectation." This time Reggie went through a demonic attack of crack cocaine use and I suffered from the side effect that came from it. We argued every day. He lied, but still came home and accused me of cheating. It was a supernatural attack of the enemy towards me even though I did not understand it. The devil was behind all of these things. His job was to get me to give up on God the Father, fall into hopelessness, then commit suicide. The word of God is true; it is His word and we must live by it. Matthew 4:4 states, "But he answered and said, It is written, Man shall not live by bread alone, but by every word that proceedeth out of the mouth of God." The problems we face no matter how horrifying they are, we should trust what God says regarding them. That's what I did.

It was doing this conference at New Bethel Church of God in Christ in Charlotte that God warned me concerning what was to come on my life. John 10;10 says, "The thief cometh not, but for to steal, and to kill, and to destroy: I am come that they might have life, and that they might have it more abundantly."

Within one month everything happened according to God's word in the Bible. At the conference I found myself at the altar. I asked God to give me His peace in my spirit because my life was chaotic. The next month I lost everything. I lost the relationship with my daughters and for three years we bounced from house to house. Reggie and I ended up living in a hotel room for two years. It was depressing and lonely but I had my faith to hold onto. I was unemployed and depended on my husband who let the devil use him.

I was put in a place where I had no other choice but to worship Him. I drew closer to God and He drew closer to me. God was with me through the process, but the devil still played me every day. He wanted me to kill myself. He told me to look at my life. I had nothing to show for it. When I was alone, he told me to jump off a bridge and end my sufferings and disappointment. But that wasn't the only voice I heard. Another voice inside of me said He would not allow me to act on it. God reminded me that His son, Jesus was tempted by Satan in an attempt to trick Him to jump off a mountain. God told me to resist the devil and he would flee from me.

In January 2015, my dependency on God paid off. I was in the hotel room with Reggie. We were out of food and had no money or transportation to get us to food. I knew Reggie was too prideful to ask anyone for help. I prayed to the Lord that I would trust Him to feed us. The next day the church van came and picked us up and on the way to Bible study, I got a call that Lee had died in the hospital. I told Patty to pick me up after church when I get back home from Bible study and I would go with her to the hospital.

After Bible study Elder Banks drove the church van. On the way home, he stopped at Food Lion and told us God said for us to shop for food and get whatever we wanted. I jumped out of the van and said, "Thank You!" to Almighty God, because He heard my prayer the day before and answered it. Even in dead places He will provide. Another time, God told me I would lose my job but not to worry about it because He would provide yet again. I had worked at a hotel for about three months and like God, said my supervisor was setting me up to be fired. God allowed me to find the schedule on the floor and my name wasn't included. I called my supervisor and let him know that I knew what he had planned. I told him he could move forward because I would not be back. The next day, a warehouse I worked at before, called me and hired me back over the phone. For me to trust God with the many uncertain times in my life paid off many times. I failed the times I neglected to seek Him and trust Him.

Trusting God through my life was all the survival skill I knew. I failed me, but He never failed me. When my children were small and we lived on Custer street, there were many shootouts and killings that went on in the community. God took care of us. One night there was a shootout across the street where I lived one of the drug dealers shot at his girlfriend right outside of my window on this same night. I hit the floor and pulled my children down with me. He covered our lives to keep the bullets from coming in and striking us. When I look back over my life I am grateful that He took care of me. There have been supernatural attacks on my life, but God always prevailed. Another time my girls need beds to sleep in. I prayed to God and told Him the bed situation belonged to him. It was His job to get them for me. The next day, when I got home from work, the next door neighbor asked if I wanted two beds she was about to throw out. All I could do at this point was thank God the Father and receive the beds. Yes, He provided again.

In order for me to heal from past hurts I had to forgive myself for the shame of my sins. I had to ask God to show me how to love me the way He did. To get out of my own way was the hardest lesson for me to learn. I had to dig down deep and look at pain and accept that I had allowed some of the dysfunction placed on my life. It was my own fault. I made bad decisions. I hold no ill will towards the abusers in my life because they were blinded by their own eternal deficiencies or else they would not have inflicted these tragic things up on me. Most of us, when we learn better, we do better.

In my case, some of my abusers repeated what had happened to them in some fashion and never knew they harmed me. The heaviness that was in my heart had to be put away just as the Lord says, "Let us lay aside every weight, and the sin which doth so easily beset us" (Hebrews 12:1). "Come unto me, all ye that labor and are heavy laden, and I will give you rest. Take my yoke upon you, and learn of me; for I am meek and lowly in heart: and ye shall find rest unto your souls"(Matthew 11:28-29).

Once I gave my pain to God I could clearly see where I had fallen short in some places in my life and was no longer ignorant of other people's schemes which really come from Satan. "Lest Satan should get an advantage of us: for we are not ignorant of his devices" (2 Corinthians 2:11, KJV).

The beautiful woman in me chose to believe the unfruitful lies told to me by others since I had no one to help me see or believe in the best me. I kept letting my pain bury me. My self-esteem would never allow me to embrace the potential and love I had inside of me. I constantly died emotionally because my surroundings said I should. The pretty inside only felt ugly. One should learn that every negative situation that comes about is temporary and it does not have to define their future. We are born as babies but we grow up and become adults. Because you have the flu today does not mean you will have it for a lifetime. There were times I starved for love and affection from others. I would have done anything to get love and affection to feel accepted, to fit in, or hear them say that approved of me.

An example of this insanity was what I did to Krystal because my mother and I were not close or I did not feel her love because of her. I did the reverse with Krystal and became too open. The relationship I had with my mother was unequally yoked and played out the same way with my two daughters. I swore to myself that I would not do the same thing to my children that my mom did with me. I didn't, but the outcome was as tragic. My mom ridiculed me by using dominance and fear. She used those tactics to keep me in check. I became timid and unsure of myself. I made Krystal my friend but that did not release me from my parenting boundaries. That was a grave mistake.

She thought she was in love, therefore, if I didn't help her see her boyfriend, she threw a fit. What kind of mother was I to do such a thing? No wonder she lost respect for me and would not listen to a word of what I said to her. She had me wrapped around her finger and she knew it. Like people say, "If I knew then what I know now." If I could go back in time and rewind what I did with her it would have been more like me beating her tail and catching a charge at the police department.

I failed again with Korean. I allowed her baby daddy to move in the house with us to keep from arguing with her about him and worrying about where she would end up if she left with him again. Children are supposed to respect what you say to them regarding certain things because you are the parent and should to know better. I was blinded by the guilt that the devil put in place to remind me of the relationship I did not have with my mother. This was another lie spawn by the devil. "If you give them what they want, your bond would be more closer. Don't you want a closer bond with them and connect like sisters in order to tell each other everything and be best buddies? You know you and your mother could never achieve this level."

I fell for this lie the same way some of the angels in heaven did, and the same way Eve did. Remember, this old dragon, the devil, Satan, Lucifer, whatever you want to call him, is the father of lies, and no truth can be found in him. He sits around looking for opportunities to destroy families and relationships. I should have rejected all negative thoughts and influence that the dragon planted in my mind. 2 Corinthians 10:4 states, "(For the weapons of our warfare are not carnal, but mighty through God to the pulling down of strong holds;)"

Guilt was the stronghold that I allowed to penetrate in my mind. At the time, I went in and out of juvenile court with both of my daughters. As a result, I did not recognize them. One cannot combat supernatural spirits with natural solutions and what I experienced was definitely from a demonic source. Ephesians 6:12 tells us "For we wrestle not against flesh and blood, but against principalities, against powers, against the rulers of the darkness of this world, against spiritual wickedness in high places." The only way to overcome any of these attacks is to stay connected to a good support system of faith believers who know how to pray and can pray with you. You need someone who can give you supportive Scripture that refers to your situation. You need someone who can speak out against the forces that may come towards your family, until you are able to do it yourself. An example of fighting the adversary and winning is when you know you're coming under attack and then ask God to help you to defeat him.

Ephesians 6 11-18 states:
"Put on the whole armour of God, that ye may be able to stand against the wiles of the devil.

For we wrestle not against flesh and blood, but against principalities, against powers, against the rulers of the darkness of this world, against spiritual wickedness in high places.

Wherefore take unto you the whole armour of God, that ye may be able to withstand in the evil day, and having done all, to stand.

Stand therefore, having your loins girt about with truth, and having on the breastplate of righteousness;

And your feet shod with the preparation of the gospel of peace;

Above all, taking the shield of faith, wherewith ye shall be able to quench all the fiery darts of the wicked.

And take the helmet of salvation, and the sword of the Spirit, which is the word of God:

Praying always with all prayer and supplication in the Spirit, and watching thereunto with all perseverance and supplication for all saints;"

Korean would curse me out with all manner of foul language when she was around 13 years old. But this time I studied the word of God with the Lord. He instructed me to anoint her toothbrush and to play a certain gospel song in her room when she went to school. I prayed, believed God and followed through with His plan. When she came home from school that day she did not speak one foul word for two weeks. She didn't know why but I did. We would still have disagreements and she would be upset with me and wanted to use the words but God closed her mouth. The devil could not use her mouth for harm, much like God shut the mouth of the lions in the den with Daniel. It would have stayed that way if I had stayed with it and been more consistent in my walk with the Lord.

There's no quick fix to the challenges that may come about in our lives, but it is important how we go through what we face. This will allow us to come out smelling like a rose and not tasting like sour grapes. During my healing, I learned to be quiet and listen for God's voice to guide me along the way. Many times I couldn't hear Him because I was too busy—talking. I thought I had to to have the last say on everything to win every argument. There is no shame in listening and being still. There is an advantage to this technique. It allows you to observe who you are dealing with and discover who they are. Are they really for you or do they want what's best for you? Or is there something they can gain to use against you for their good?

Also, if you move in silence, no one can get next to you and learn your next move. It's like if you are getting ready to fight an enemy, you don't say to the enemy, "Now I'm going to slap you in the face and kick you," then proceed to do exactly what you said. They will have the upper hand because they know what you are about to do to them. When you keep quiet you keep them guessing. This way your enemy cannot set you up for a fall. The wisdom I learned from being quiet has become priceless to me. Knowing when and when not to speak come with great gifts.

James 1:19 tells us, "Wherefore, my beloved brethren, let every man be swift to hear, slow to speak, slow to wrath:" God had to show me my emotions were fickle, temporary, and not to be trusted. When negative feelings came up, I did not have to quickly act on them, but I needed to meditate on what was said and how would respond. The more slack I was in my relationship with God, the more undefeated I became in my life. I learned to trust God and believe in His word. Another trick dressed up by the devil was "people pleasing." It doesn't matter if it is your own family, spouse, children, friends, co-workers, lovers, etc. If it is not fruitful or good for your own spirit, it is not pleasing to God. "For do I now persuade men, or God? or do I seek to please men? for if I yet pleased men, I should not be the servant of Christ" (Galatians 1:10).

When my daughters went through puberty, it was a perilous time for me as a single mother. Just because you are a parent at any age doesn't mean you know how to parent successfully. With myself, I only had one part of the parenting component—the financial. I lacked the emotional and structural balance to become effective. When you "people please," you have a form of godliness and don't have a clue of who you are or whose you are. I was angry and not happy with my life.

As I expressed earlier, I allowed my past and present situation to kill me. In a way, Satan had fun with me. Even though I was not physically dead, I was mentally deceased. I had sold out to my children and other people's needs and wants and put myself last. I became the devil's pawn and he played me on the game board every chance he got. I was his slave and at his every beck and call. All anyone had to do was play on my need for attention and affection and they had me. Even with my love for God, I was set up and used because some of the people around me acted like they loved God in order to stay with me or to lay with me.

A parent cannot be too strict or one cannot be too lenient. There must be balance for it to work. My hungry and thirst for wanting a daddy in my life and the lives of my daughters, led me to participate in some unhealthy relationships. The familiar negativism mirrored how I was raised as a child. Both of my daughters suffered from not having a father in the home. Krystal became sexually promiscuous at an early age and Korean always dated men who were eight to ten years older.

This generational curse of fatherless men in my family bothers me because I don't want my grandchildren or anyone for that matter to experience this. Hopefully, they can learn from my story. Having both parents in the home brings about balance to a child's life if the relationship with the parents are healthy. However, I know in this day and time, it may not be possible.

According to goodhousekeeping.com, 30 to 40 percent of marriages end in divorce. Regardless, do not stay in a domestically abusive relationship. It's not all physically. If a person requires all of your time and separates you from your family and friends, and don't want you to have time for yourself, that's a warning sign. If a person screams and curses at you whether in private or in public, that's a warning sign. If a person makes you feel as if you have to choose between them and your own children, that's a warning sign. If a person makes you feel guilty for spending time with anybody other than them, that's a warning sign. Because of the sake of family, I ignored all of the signs and it cost me greatly. If you're in an unhealthy relationship or marriage, whether or not children are involved, get out of it. Find someone who can teach you what makes a good solid relationship.

Now that I'm a grandmother, I have set out to break this fatherless curse for my grandchildren by teaching them what is right. When it comes down to it, you must respect yourself and others. I try to teach them sound values about life. They need to know by example what being a positive parent is about. When it's their time to parent, I want them to have great examples. The evilness of this world will take anyone. No one is exempt from its fury. I spend time asking them questions about sex and self-esteem issues, and I help them to understand they can be anything they want to be if they believed it in their hearts. I wish I had someone who invested time talking to me regarding life and what to expect. This is why I believe it is my mission with my grandchildren to fill in any gaps my daughters may have left out. If they don't feel comfortable with their mothers, they can ask me.

During my childhood there were a few special people who showed me they cared. My eight grade math and science teacher, Mr. Williams showed me what I didn't see in myself. He understood some of my challenges and gave me my first little job, helping him to grade some of his school papers. He saw I had a caring heart and suggested I become a nurse. Later, I did. My spiritual mentor, Evan E. Moore, was a woman who loved on me like a true sister. She allowed me to work in her salon as a shampoo stylist and taught me the importance of recognizing the spiritual attacks hidden by the enemy. Because of her love and guidance, I am the proud warrior I am today. I love her dearly. My prayer partner is a lovely young woman by the name of Shirlon Hurd. She is a true blessing and a wonderful person who has been down in the valley helping me with my prayer requests. I am forever grateful to her for her strength. My cousin, Johnny Mae Reed, is the best family member I've ever known. She is another prayer warrior who got down in the trenches of life with me to help me become victorious. Her kind spirit and loving heart let me know I could trust her with my life's deepest secrets.

Recently, I had the pleasure of knowing a phenomenal woman, Rosemary Bristol, who is also beautiful inside and out. I love her tremendously and her heart matches mine in the way she gives of herself without selfishness. Everything that has happened in my life shows me that I am more together than most people who fret over meaningless things that aren't worth complaining about. The Good Lord made me the person I am; a strong tower who no one can be compared to, a lady warrior who had to fight her whole life to keep her head above water. When the hard times pressed in on my mind, the Holy Spirit brought all the strength of truth to aid me in my survival of whatever trail I faced at the time. It was for the glory of God Almighty that I was able to withstand such abuse because He was right there with me even when I could not hear Him, tell Him, or see Him. Because Jesus lives in me,

I can conquer anything I've had to endure.

He asked me, "Must I suffer alone that you may not?"

The Bible tells us that afflictions and persecution will be many but, it is how we deal with them that makes the difference. "When thou passest through the waters, I will be with thee; and through the rivers, they shall not overflow thee: when thou walkest through the fire, thou shalt not be burned; neither shall the flame kindle upon thee" (Isaiah 43:2).

My heart is immensely grateful to God our Father and His son, Jesus Christ for allowing me to walk in these many dark places in my life to break the yolks of bondage off my life as well as others through my transparency. If I survived all of this adversity and travails on every side, you can, too.

The healing God put on my heart restored my life because I can address everyone in my past who did any ill towards me with a pure heart of love and compassion. If any one of them ever needed me again, I would be there because it is not about what they inflicted upon me. I can still love them because it was never about them and their hiccups. It is all about the mighty name of Jesus who shed his blood for us to know how to love unconditionally as He did. The things that happened hurt me but t my living has not been in vain. We have all been tricked by the devil but God can show you a different way to hold your head up high. Your present circumstances do not define the person you will become. In all things I give thanks to Him for allowing me to soar like an eagle and be protected under His wings. God was where the chilly winds do not blow. Our lives are seasonal. If not, we would have been stuck in some of these areas. I know because now I'm blessed, happy, no longer homeless, working, can move my limbs, clothed, and in my right mind.

Made in the USA
Columbia, SC
09 August 2020

15885460R00107